WAKE UP CHURCH!

WAKE UP CHURCH!

It's Time to
Take My Light into the World!

2nd EDITION

Patricia S. Welsh

Leavitt Peak Press

ISBN: 978-1-961017-81-8 (sc)
ISBN: 978-1-961017-82-5 (e)

Rev. date: 07/24/2023

A MARVELOUS THING

I'm just a speck in Your creation,
But You know me on a personal basis.
You know my heart and what I do,
And can pick me out from all earthly faces.

It blows my mind that the Creator of all
Wants to have one-on-one time with me.
You tell me that I'm Your precious child,
And I'm a part of Your royal family.

You have pulled me up out of the muck
And put me on solid ground.
You've washed me up, by the blood of Jesus,
And with royalty I have been crowned!

Oh, what a marvelous thing it is
To know the victory that's been won;
Not by my own feeble efforts,
But by the act of Your precious Son!

- Patricia S. Welsh
© February 2020

CONTENTS

FOREWORD

Dear Reader,

It is an honor to share this amazing book with you. Can you imagine God talking to you personally and you writing down what He is saying to you? Can you envision conversing with Him, laughing with Him, and understanding how real, personable, caring and compassionate He is? I think you will be glad to know how much He loves you. Yes, You!

This book is one with the Lord—the living word—a first-hand experience ordained by God for you. How blessed we are to read this book, because it explains how important we are to God, our creator.

Our Father God, Jesus Christ, and The Holy Spirit speak to you and help you understand God's love. God knows everything about you. Every person created and conceived has a purpose, and every person matters to Him.

"Before you were born, I set you apart, I appointed you as a prophet to the nations." Jeremiah 1:5 NLT

This book contains a powerful message from God to his people. He has given Patricia S. Welsh His friendship, an understanding, and the ability to pen this beautiful inspirational message.

The Holy Spirit helps us establish a spiritual relationship with the Lord, so that we can teach in the marketplace and get His message of love to those with an ear to hear and a foot to follow. The journey has just begun, but time is very, very short! We must make it a priority to take His light out into the world right now!

I pray that as you read this book you will be enlightened and let the word of God dwell in you richly in all wisdom.

"Let the word of Christ dwell in you richly in all wisdom; teaching and admonishing one another in psalms and hymns and spiritual songs, singing with grace in your hearts to the Lord." –Colossians 3:16 & Romans 15:13 KJV

Remember, our faith is the victory that overcomes the spirit of the world.

"for everyone born of God overcomes the world. This is the victory that has overcome the world, even our faith." 1 John 5:4.

The journey begins by taking the first step. Enjoy!"

May God richly bless you,

Rosann Pavlov

Stay vigilant.

INTRODUCTION

Did you ever think to yourself that there must be something more; that the "Church", Jesus' Ekklesia, in His time was so different than what you experience in church today? Did you ever wonder why it's so hard to know what your purpose is; to do what you think you're supposed to do; that the scriptures you read don't make sense based on what you've learned in church?

These are all questions that I've asked myself over the years. In 2009 I started a quest to find the answers to those questions. I watched many videos and heard many recordings of people who seem to have confidence in who they are in Christ, what their purpose is and actively showing God's love to the people around them. I asked God to show me how to have what they have. His reply through scripture was, **"Seek Me first."**

My first thought was how do I do that? The second thought was what does that even mean? I read a comment by someone that said you must have a personal relationship with God, and one of the best ways to do that is to journal; to set a specific time of day to spend time with the Lord, to pray and listen for His still, quiet voice, then write down what He says.

Journaling wasn't something I had an interest in doing, so I tabled that. But, as time went on and I still didn't have a breakthrough, I decided to give it a try. The results have been astonishing.

For over a year, I have been keeping journals of my thoughts and conversations with God. I've labeled them "My Time With God". That's what it is; time I've committed to praise and worship God, to quiet my mind and listen to His quiet, calm voice. At first, that was the most difficult part of our time together, calming my mind and activating my spirit so I could commune (spend time) with Him. It gets easier the more you do it.

It's amazing the topics we've covered, the visions I've seen, and the poems, drawings and paintings that I've envisioned. He is an amazing God; *so much more than we've been led to believe!* It astonishes me the truths in the Bible that no one ever told me about or had explained to me. I call them the hidden truths of the Bible. That is exactly what they are, truths hidden by Satan's deception, lies, and his infiltration in the modern day church.

One of our conversations dealt with that very topic. God was explaining something to me and I asked Him, "Why was I never taught this before? I'm 67 years old." I grew up in the church. God's answer was this,

"Well, because Satan doesn't want you to know this stuff. He's infiltrated the Church, spoke his lies, and people have believed them."

For the last decade, God has been showing me and teaching me how to be a true disciple of Jesus. It's been a blessing beyond anything I could have imagined. God, Creator of everything, wants to have a personal relationship with me. Who am I? It reminds me of what David said in Psalm 8:3-4: **"When I look at your heavens, the work of your fingers, the moon and the stars, which You have set in place, what is man that You are mindful of him . . ."**

David, as I, was amazed that God would even consider us, let alone give us dominion over the works of His hand, over everything of this earth.

God's message to ALL people is this:

He, God of everything, loves us, is concerned about us, wants to spend time with us, take care of us and wants to bless us beyond measure. He wants a personal relationship with EVERY person.

Wow, how awesome is that?

I think it would be fair to say that most of God's people really don't have a true sense of how to be a disciple of God. They don't know how to have a personal relationship with Him, to understand what exactly happened when Jesus suffered and died for us and WHY. They don't know what God's will is and how to do it, and more importantly, how to tell others about God, and do what Jesus did and more.

Through my journals, God has been teaching me these things and now wants to teach them to you, through this book. He has conveyed a very important message to His Church. He loves His Church, but He's not really happy with us right now. In fact, he's very disappointed.

He wants to save a billion people in this last great worldwide revival, and He needs His Church to step up and take His message and LOVE to the world. Unfortunately, most of us are asleep at the wheel. We are NOT being "little Christs" to the world, and that is what we Christians are supposed to be.

My hope for this book is that it will rekindle your faith, inspire you, and help you understand what being a disciple of God really is. I hope you'll have a deep personal relationship with Him in which you can intimately talk with each other, so that He can teach you, guide you, comfort you, and show you just how deeply He loves and cherishes you, bringing amazing insights and wonders into your life.

In case you believe, or have been taught, that God doesn't talk to individual people, it says differently in John 16:13,

"When the Spirit of Truth comes, he will guide you into all the truth, for he will not speak on his own authority, but whatever he hears he will speak, and he will declare to you the things that are to come."

I hope that you will take His message and love out into the world and make a huge difference in people's lives. We need to do it now. We are running out of time.

As God keeps telling me:

WAKE UP CHURCH, TIME IS VERY SHORT!!

I'm grateful, and humbled, that God has chosen me to bring His message of Love to you. It is a great honor, but also daunting. Who am I? However, He knows me better than I know myself. . .

So, okay God; Your will be done, Your words written; and thanks for never giving up on us!

- Patricia S. Welsh

AUTHOR'S NOTE

Throughout this book the reader will see numerous quotes that come from conversations I had with God. His statements will be in italics and mine in regular print.

Even though God spoke directly to me in my journals, answering my questions, and helping me, He wants me to tell you that the messages in my journals are for you, too.

When you read this book, imagine that God is talking directly to you because His message IS for you.

CHAPTER 1

GETTING TO KNOW GOD

How long did it take you to know your best friend? Did it happen the first day you decided to start a friendship? No. It took time to get to know, to understand and completely trust that person. The longer you're together, the stronger your bond is, the deeper your relationship. It's the same with God.

Whether you've been a Christian for a long time, like me, or have given your life to Jesus recently, the most important thing to do is to get to know Him.

Why He Wants Us to Know Him

WE WERE CREATED TO HAVE FELLOWSHIP WITH HIM. This is what He told me,

"I created everyone so that I could commune with you all and take care of you. . . I love all of my creation, especially humans, for you were created to be with me."

The Biblical meaning of commune is this:

"Commune" means to focus on God, converse, talk, often with profound intensity, intimate communication or

rapport as sharing your heart and mind with God in prayer: an interchange of ideas or sentiments, derived from French "comun" meaning – common, to share.[1]

I'm glad commune is derived from a word that means common, because that's what I am. I am not some special, big important person in the world. However, I *am* important to God, *just as you.*

HE LONGS FOR A PERSONAL RELATIONSHIP WITH EVERY SINGLE ONE OF US. That is why He sent His son to earth to become the Redeemer, the Messiah for us all, for *every* human being. Jesus became the bridge between God and us and made it possible for humans to commune with Him and have a personal relationship again. That is only possible through His Holy Spirit. God told me,

My Son came to earth as a human and lived as a man so that he could become the atonement for humankind's sins. When he did that, he made it possible for human's spirits to connect with my Spirit so they can come back to me and experience eternity again, so they can have a personal relationship with me.

HE YEARNS FOR US TO GIVE HIM OUR HEARTS, not just to profess that He is our God. He wants to take care of us.

When I started journaling, most of God's messages were about His love and care for us. In His very first message to me, He spoke of this.

Giving your heart to me means being still and knowing that I AM God, and ALSO knowing that I love you no matter what you do or don't do.

He longs for us to love Him back through a personal relationship with Him.

GOD MISSES US! He misses our spiritual interaction. He mentioned this to me in one of our conversations.

Most people are too busy or too lazy to have a personal relationship with me . . . that breaks my heart. How would you feel if you loved someone and they stopped calling, never spent time with you, never asked how you were doing or how you were feeling? What if that person never made an effort to communicate with you, unless they wanted something from you? Well, that's how I feel.

HE WANTS US TO DO HIS WILL so that others can be saved. We have to know Him to know what His will is. He told me,

My people can only know my will by developing their spiritual senses. The Bible tells what my will is, but my people will not understand it if they only use their carnal minds when they read. The Truth is revealed by Holy Spirit and He can only do that through someone's spirit.

One of the hardest things for me to grasp, even though I've been a Christian over five decades, is the fact that God thinks I'm worthy to have a relationship with Him. Often times, we, His own people, don't think we are worthy enough to stand in His presence, let alone have a personal relationship with Him. Nevertheless, He addressed that in a message to me.

You always seem surprised when we tell you how much you mean to us, how beautiful and precious you are to us.

(Note: God often uses the pronoun "us"; as a triune God.)

It's as if you don't feel worthy enough to be cared for by us, to be loved by us.

I told Him that maybe that was in the back of my mind; that after all, He was the God of everything! He responded,

Yes, but I AM also your Father, who loves you with all my being; a father who cherishes you, a father who loves spending time with you, a father who is proud to call you daughter.

3

What a remarkable statement! **We are a part of God's family; we are royalty!** This is something that most of us have never been taught; we don't understand that He isn't just our God, but is also our spiritual Father. He has adopted us into His royal family, and we have all the rights of a child of God, just like Jesus. We even have the same authority that Jesus has. Authority is one of the things He gave us when He exchanged His righteousness for our sin.

God wants us to use that authority to make a difference in the world. That is what His will is. (He will delve deeper into that later.) It can be frightening going into the world and telling others about God and showing His love for them. He understands that, but He also knows we can do it *with* Him. He stated that to me.

Show others my heart through yours. I will be with you always, and nothing is impossible with me!

We are not alone when we go into the world. He is always with us. Nothing is impossible for Him, which means that nothing is impossible for us if we truly have given our lives to Him.

(Note: I never quite understood the triune God concept. I had to check for verses that confirm that He does indeed often use plural pronouns when referring to Himself.)

Genesis 1:26 says, "**Then God said, "Let us make man in our image, after our likeness . . .**" Similar plural pronouns are used in Genesis 3:22; 11:7; and in Isaiah6:8

Understanding Who God Is

We need to have confidence in Him, which means we need to understand who He is.

HE IS SUPREME GOD

Three attributes show that God **IS** God:

1. Omniscience – (all knowing) He knows everything.

2. Omnipotence – (all powerful) He can do anything.

3. Omni benevolence – (supremely good) He is perfectly good.

This is how He explained it to me:

I AM.

What a powerful statement. He is all. He is everything. Then God added something that explained who He is in context of the conversation we were having. *I AM the same now, before, and forever.*

I think it's interesting to note that in our conversations, when we are talking about anything that pertains to God's character, he will capitalize the word AM as opposed to a statement about what He will do. *I am going to take care of that problem.*

The above mentioned attributes show us who God is as a powerful God ruler, but it doesn't really convince us that He is someone we want to know on a personal level, or that we're worthy to know on a personal level. We must look at some of His other attributes to be able to do that.

The following scriptures define other attributes of God that show Him as a personable being:

HE IS HONORABLE: Psalm 25:8 says, **"Good and upright is the Lord."** Honor is part of God's character. He has the highest moral standard and integrity. He will not compromise His principles. That is good to know because that means we can trust what He says.

He's not fickle, doesn't change as regards to His loyalties, interests or affection. He means what He says. He never contradicts Himself like some people that we know who say something one day and something different later. Such as when parents make a "promise" to their child and then later change their minds.

HE IS LOVE: I John 4:8 mentions this. **"Anyone who does not love, does not know God, for God is love".** Love is another attribute of God. One thing you must understand is this: God and His attributes are not separate; they are part of who He is: His character. He told me this,

Love is the driving force behind everything we do. Love is our nature, so it has to be the driving force; it can't NOT be. You cannot separate love from us, because love is who we are.

God's love isn't like the world's love, which is based on emotions, someone's feeling, circumstances or if we like someone or not. His love is unconditional; it's not based on conditions like the world's love.

Have you ever had anyone tell you that they love you, then later tell you that they don't ever want to see you again because you said something they didn't like? Well, that's a good example of CONDITIONAL love.

God's love is based on His character: He loves: simple and to the point. It's not based on His feelings or on ours. It doesn't matter what we do or don't do, or what others do or don't do to us. He loves. That fact, that Truth, is something that we can count on, which is a great foundation for a strong personal relationship with Him, just as you would have with a best friend. As He told me,

We love you! You are a treasure to us. Thank you for opening your heart to us. We know your struggles, and we are always here to help you. Keep trusting us and remember that all things are possible through us.

HE IS RIGHTEOUS: The scripture Psalm 11:7 says,

"For the Lord is righteous; He loves righteous deeds; the upright shall behold His face."

Righteousness is another one of God's attributes, just like honor. He will always do right. He won't be swayed. He is faithful to those that live righteously, as said in Psalm 34:15, 17

"The eyes of the Lord are toward the righteous, and His ears are toward their cry. When the righteous cry for help the Lord hears and delivers them out of all their troubles."

God's righteousness is what Jesus exchanged for our sin. *Righteousness is an attribute that belongs to God. It is a gift from God to humanity through His love: it is the God-given quality imputed (credited) to mankind upon believing in the Son of God.*[2]

In other words, we become righteous when we believe in Jesus and accept His righteousness in exchange for our sins.

I never quite understood what that meant until God explained it to me in one of our conversations.

(Note: I am going to write the conversation as it occurred. His words will be in *italics*, mine in normal font.)

> *Notice in the above definition it says that righteousness is a gift from me to you through my love.*

> Yes, I see that.

7

Well, what have I told you about my love?

That it is a part of You, Your nature.

Yes, it is who I AM. Love cannot be separated from me.

Oh, wow . . . this is amazing . . . so when we receive righteousness from Jesus through Your love, we are actually receiving You!

Yes. I can't be separated from my love or my righteousness. So I ask you, why did my Son give his righteousness to you when he took your sin?

Because his righteousness is You?

And . . . ?

Uh . . . Oh, You and sin cannot exist together.

Correct. He HAD to give his righteousness away because he took your sin and it can't exist where I am. My Shekhina Glory would have destroyed it, which would have destroyed my Son as well. Since he gave me to you in place of your sin, you are now worthy to spend eternity with me, because we are one in spirit. You are no longer unholy; you are holy because you belong to me, you are a part of me, and I of you. We are family.

Wow, isn't that awesome? This explains what Colossians 3:9-11 means.

"Do not lie to each other, seeing that you have put off the old self with its practices and have put on the new self, which is being renewed in knowledge *after the image of its Creator*. Here there is no Gentile or Jew, circumcised

8

or uncircumcised, barbarian, **Scythian, slave or free, but Christ is all and in all."** (Italics added.)

In other words, those of us that have accepted Jesus' righteousness (God) have now become one nation under God, His nation, a part of His royal family! We are all brothers and sisters, but we are also one with each other through the Holy Spirit. Now *that* is about as personal as you can get.

(NOTE: Jesus can be with Father God now because our sins were buried with Him when He was put in the tomb. When He rose from the dead, our sins stayed there – dead.)

HE IS JUST AND FAITHFUL: Psalm 89:14 says, **"Righteousness and justice are the foundation of Your throne; steadfast love and faithfulness go before You."** Proverbs 2:8 states, **"[He is] guarding the paths of justice, and watching over the way of His saints."**

God will never compromise His standards. He shows no partiality. His judgment is fair and has the same standard for everyone: the righteousness of Jesus. When He gives His verdict, He bases it on that one thing: Is that person a reflection of Jesus. Jesus is the standard and our example of the way we should live.

Let's look at the modern day judicial system as an example of the following concept: It's obvious that there is often a double standard. If you are famous, or very rich, or know someone in high places, or can afford to pay someone off, then you often get exonerated when the average person would go to prison for the same offense. It gets very frustrating because it is not fair.

However, with God, the standard is the same for all and the penalty is the same for everyone. He never changes the rules.

HE IS GENEROUS: As stated in Philippians 4:19, "**And God will supply every need of yours according to His riches in glory by Christ Jesus.**"

We had a conversation about how He wants to bless people, but can't because of their unwillingness to grab hold of His blessings. He was frustrated.

My people don't ask for enough. I have many blessings to give to them but most aren't delivered. How sad is that? Many of my people think it's selfish to ask for more blessings, but that's looking at it from a carnal perspective, a human point-of-view. Look at it from MY point-of-view. I give because I AM a good Father. I get great pleasure in blessing my people! But, my blessings are two-fold: they aren't just to make my people "rich", but also to pass on and share with others.

We are to share the blessings God has given us. When we do, we are helping to right the wrongs in people's lives. For example: Hunger is part of Satan's curse. When you give food to someone who is starving, you are righting the wrong caused by Satan's evil. But if you give them the opportunity to grow their own food, you are able to change the circumstances of that person's life because Jesus redeemed our authority and broke the curse. People do not have to live under the curse any more.

A God who cares for others and us is worth getting to know on a personal basis. *What other amazing things does He have in store for us?*

There were two main ideas God kept restating in my first journal: *He loves us unconditionally, and with Him, nothing is impossible; together we can do anything because everything is possible.*

The problem with us is that we often don't act like royal children of God. We are timid, anxious and sometimes fearful. We look like and act like the people of the world. There is no difference between us. I remember a saying that was popular years ago: *If we were arrested for being a Christian, would there be enough evidence to convict us?* Unfortunately, for most of the people in the modern church (us) the answer would be, "No."

Are the children of earthly royal backgrounds timid and afraid? No, they are confident in their identities as children of the king. All their needs are met, and they have the authority of the king because they are his children, his heirs.

Well, we, God's Children, are heirs of His kingdom. We have everything we need and His authority, because we are His children. It's time we acted like it. We need to confidently take our authority and make a difference in the world. That is our destiny, our purpose. The following message that He gave to me reiterates that:

As a child of mine you need to be living from your spiritual mind and senses. You are a part of us and we of you. We are now one. Your old selves were buried with my Son and you were raised in him and are brand new people. The old things are gone.

I had a vision that dealt with this:

> I shut my eyes and I saw people taking Jesus into the tomb, and when they sealed Him in, my vision went dark. It was total blackness. All of a sudden, there was light and I was sitting with Jesus on the slab in the tomb. He was holding my hand. He turned His head and looked at me, and we both had huge grins on our faces. He said, "Let's go!" and we did. We just took off and flew. Well, soared would be a better word. We soared like eagles. It was magnificent! Our spirits were joined together.

If you don't live from your spirit you could suffer needlessly, because suffering is often the consequence of ignoring the Truth of God and listening to Satan's lies and deceptions. Anyone who chooses to live from their carnal mind instead of their spiritual mind powered by God's Spirit, could suffer some very harmful consequences. God doesn't put that harm on people, it's simply the aftereffects of them not living according to the divine plan of the Creator.

We have no authority over the world if we aren't turned on to the Holy Spirit, because it's through the Holy Spirit that our authority and power are activated.

Compare this to an electric circuit in your house. There is a light bulb. No light comes from the bulb until it's connected to a power source. When you wire the bulb to a power source, through a switch, the bulb and power source are now connected. However, until the switch is turned on, there is no power getting to the bulb. We must turn the switch on to light up the bulb.

You are the bulb. God is the power source. The Holy Spirit is the wire running from the power source to the switch. Your spirit is the wire running from the switch to you, the bulb. The switch is your will. You use your will to switch from the carnal mind to the spiritual mind. In the OFF position, you are controlled by your carnal mind. In the ON position, power from God flows through Holy Spirit into your spirit which allows God's light to shine through you. You use your will to turn off the switch as well, which stops the flow of God's power. You are still connected, because you gave your life to Jesus and was wired to Holy Spirit, but there's no power; not until you turn on the switch.

When we have a personal relationship with God, we are connected to His Spirit, and we have every benefit that comes with it. If our switch is turned on, then we have the power to reason like Him, do what He does, and we can use our authority over everything in the world that He has authority over.

He told me:

You are above everything in this world because you are my child. You have authority over everything in the carnal realm, because I gave Yeshua my authority and he has given it to you.

(Note: God often uses the Hebrew name of His son.)

We want to surround you with our love and renew your mind. You are precious to us and are a very important part of what we want to accomplish on earth. You are a part of us now. You are in us and we are in you. Together we can do anything!

What an amazing promise! Having a personal relationship with God is what we've been searching for our whole lives. We just don't realize it.

Knowing the attributes of God and hearing from his own words how He loves us and wants to take care of us, and understanding what Jesus accomplished when He sacrificed himself on our behalf, gives us the sense that we are worthy enough to have a personal relationship with God. It instills in us the desire to know Him better.

(Author's Note: After each section there is a Bible verse that pertains to what was written in that section. There is also a prayer. Read it aloud as a prayer from you to God.)

I John 3:1

"See what kind of love the Father has given to us, that we should be called children of God."

I thank You God, that You want to have a personal relationship with me, that I am worthy to be called Your child. Help me Holy Spirit, to know who I am in Christ, to understand what being a child of God really means. Help me to understand, Lord, what Your unconditional love really is. I want to understand all that You're saying so I can step out in faith and make a difference in the world. I love You Lord!

Truths That Must Be Understood

Truth allows us to make good decisions that benefit us, not harm us. Here are truths that we should understand before we can commit ourselves to a lasting relationship with God.

FAITH IS THE CATALYST - Before we can even talk about having a personal relationship with God, we must have faith. What is faith?

Hebrews 11:1 says, "**Faith is the assurance of things hoped for, the conviction of things not seen.**"

Faith is having confidence that what God has said in His word will happen in the physical realm, because it *already* has happened in the spiritual realm. God told me this one day:

Faith is a must, because the carnal mind will seek carnal solutions to carnal (earthly) problems. People need to activate their spiritual senses by having faith in my Word; calling forth what ISN'T, so it can become what IS in the natural realm. That's what it means to have my will be done on earth as it is in heaven. I have authority over the earth, but it manifests when a human verbally declares it in faith."

Without faith, we could not even be a Christian, as Hebrew 11:6 states, "**And without faith it is impossible to please Him, for whoever would draw near to God must believe that He exists and that He rewards those that [diligently] seek Him.**"

We can't just believe that He exists. Satan believes that. We must also believe that there are benefits of being a disciple of God, and that our lives will be changed for the better because of those benefits. That takes faith.

Faith comes from the Holy Spirit and when we invite Jesus into our hearts, His Spirit then gives us the faith we need to enable us to believe that God *IS*, and that He loves us. It is faith that gives us confidence to have a personal relationship with Him. One of the definitions of faith says this,

Faith: Complete trust or confidence in someone or something.

When we seek a personal relationship with God, we are putting our trust in Him and His willingness to take care of us. He reminded me of this in one of our conversations:

Trust me. I love you. I want the best for you—ALL that I have for you. Oh how I want to bless my people!

We talked before about how Jesus exchanged His righteousness for our sin, but to have a personal relationship with God, we must understand the rest of the story.

THE LOST CONNECTION - The reason Jesus had to be the Redeemer Is that humans lost their connection with God when Adam and Eve sinned. That connection was the spiritual connection. This is another area that most of God's people don't understand. We know that Adam and Eve sinned and then were banished from the garden, but what we fail to understand is the underlying consequence: separation from God. I'll let God explain it to you, from a conversation we had.

My people do not understand what Yeshua accomplished with his suffering and death.

You must understand the correlation between what Adam did and what Yeshua did. Most of my people don't really understand this. They understand the "what" but not the "how". You have to understand the "how". How did Adam sin? It didn't exist in the world until Adam focused his attention on the physical realm instead of the spiritual realm.

We had a wonderful relationship prior to that point. My Holy Spirit sustained him and I gave him my authority over everything in the world. He was spirit, but I gave him a human body so he could interact in the world, but he lived by his spirit, which was according to my divine plan. His thoughts were on me, as my thoughts were on him.

When Adam and Eve focused their thoughts on the serpent's lies, they stopped reasoning with their spirits and started thinking with their carnal mind.

(Note: "Carnal" is relating to physical needs and activities, not the spiritual.)

As a result, Adam and Eve ate from the Tree of Knowledge of Good and Evil. They had chosen Evil. Consequently, I had to remove my Spirit from them because sin cannot exist in my presence.

As a divine Holy being, it is impossible for God to exist with sin. Wherever God's manifest presence is, His Glory, anything unholy has to realign with His divine plan, restored to the original design.

For instance: If someone has a deformed hand and God's Glory, shows up (His manifest presence), that hand would have to realign to the original divine plan, which is wholeness. There is an example of this in Matthew 12:10-13.

On the Sabbath, Jesus went to the synagogue and there was a man there with a withered hand. The Pharisees asked Jesus if it was lawful to heal on the Sabbath. They were trying to trap Him so that they could accuse Him. He responded by saying that if they had a sheep that had fallen into a pit on the Sabbath, they would go save it. He then said, in Matthew 12:13,

"How much more value is a man than a sheep! So it is lawful to do good on the Sabbath." Then He said to the man, "Stretch out your hand". And the man stretched it out, and it was restored healthy, like the other."

Jesus had God's righteousness, His holiness, and was able to call forth God's Glory, His presence, into the situation because He had God's authority. As a result, the hand had to realign with God's divine plan.

When God's manifest presence shows up where there is sin, it has to die. Why? There was no sin in the original divine plan. This is why Jesus had to take our sins upon Himself when He gave us God's righteousness. *(Remember: when Jesus gave us righteousness, He was giving us God.)* If Jesus hadn't taken humankind's sins upon Himself, any person that would decide to accept His righteousness would die because the sin in that person would have to realign to the original divine plan. God told me,

If I hadn't removed my Spirit from Adam and Eve when they sinned, the consuming fire of my Glory, my Holiness, would have destroyed the sin, which would have destroyed my beloved creation and I didn't want that to happen.

After that, Adam and Eve had to rely on their carnal minds to be able to cope in the physical realm without my Spirit. They didn't lose their spirits or authority. Their spirits became disconnected from me and, unfortunately, from then on they used their authority, under the influence of Satan, to advance worldly things, not spiritual things. Sadly, all of those worldly things can lead to death, eternal separation from me.

Most people don't understand that we are spiritual beings first, but living in a physical body, an earth suit. This is what God had to say about that:

A personal relationship with me has to be spiritual because I am not human. I can't interact in the world because I have no carnal body, no earth suit. I AM Spirit. You are spirit, too, but you also have a carnal body and mind. You need them to interact in the world.

 I was very confused about this until God explained it to me in a conversation we had:

> *Your essence is spiritual. It's there all the time, it's eternal. But your human nature thinks that the physical and spiritual conditions are separate; they're not. Your spirit is who you are. Your body is like a suit; one you wear to be able to interact in the world, kind of like a space suit.*
>
> *If your spirit would leave, the body would collapse. What do you think happens when someone dies? Their spirit, their essence leaves and the body collapses and begins to decompose. However, if their spirit comes back, they put on the earth suit again and it's good once more; think of Lazareth.*

Lazareth was a man Jesus raised from the dead. You can read about it in John 11:33-44. He continued.

> The spirit doesn't need a body to exist, but a body needs
> a spirit to exist.

In the book, *Pushing the Boundaries in Christ*, Tony Meyers says that we, as children of God, are meant to interact with the physical world, NOT to be constrained by it and its limitations.[3] (Remember, we do not have to live under the curse anymore.) God agreed with Tony:

Absolutely, as my child, you have no natural boundaries. Your body is bound by the natural laws, which explains why the body decays when your spirit, your essence, leaves. However, when your spirit is in your body, your spirit has authority over your body as long as you are turned on to my Holy Spirit.

As Tony has said, you have to change your thinking. You are not a mere mortal under physical limitations, you also live from the spiritual realm; you are my child! Live like it! Everything I have is yours, MY mind, MY heart, MY traits, MY blessings, and My Spirit living in you. Anything is possible!

You have my authority, so you have authority over everything of the natural world as well as in the spiritual realm. I didn't take authority from Adam and Eve when they sinned. They more or less gave Satan the control over it. However, Yeshua redeemed humankind's authority, so now you can use it whenever you need to.

(NOTE: Jesus didn't come just to redeem people, but all that was lost; everything under Satan's curse. That includes our authority, the marketplace, homes, businesses, schools, governments, cities, and eventually, nations.)

Matthew 28:18-19 mentions this. "**And Jesus came and said to them, "All authority in heaven and on earth has been given to me. Go therefore and make disciples of all nations . . ."**

The following verses, Revelation 21:23-24, talk about the New Jerusalem and who will come into the city.

"The city does not need the sun or the moon to shine on it, because God's glory illuminates it, and its lamp is the Lamb. The nations will walk in its light, and the kings of the earth will bring their glory into it."

What is the glory of the kings? It is God's Glory within the redeemed nations.

Tony commented that we were never created to be dependent on the world. We were created as humans to interact with the world, but to be dependent on God; just like Adam and Eve in the Garden of Eden.

One thing that you have to understand is that God exists in Eternity in the spiritual realm. There is no beginning or ending, because TIME doesn't exist there. Everything happens NOW. When He created trees they didn't grow over a period of years, they just appeared NOW, when He called them forth into the physical realm. He can see the past, present and future all at the same time. He sees everything NOW. He lives from the NOW. In the Garden, Adam and Eve lived from the NOW, in the spiritual realm. They lived in Eternity, TIME did not affect them.

When Adam and Eve sinned, they fell into a TIMELINE. Why? They lost their connection to God in the spiritual realm. In the physical realm, TIME is required so things don't all happen at the same time. Time gave Adam and Eve a chance for redemption. If they had not fallen into a timeline, they would have immediately died with no chance of repenting. Death is the consequence of sin.

TIME has a beginning and an ending, a timeline. Adam and Eve's timelines didn't start when they were conceived. It started when they sinned. Our timelines start when we are conceived, because we are the seed of Adam; we have his sinful nature.

When do our timelines end? Remember, TIME makes redemption possible. Redemption is the end of our timelines. Sin, from the physical realm, is removed and replaced with God in Eternity, the spiritual realm, when we're redeemed. We have the spiritual connection with God again and, through our spirits, live in the NOW.

When we live in the NOW, eternity (the spiritual realm), we are not bound by time because we have been redeemed. We don't have to wait until we leave this earth and go to heaven to get our blessings. We can have them NOW. We are not conformed to this world.

A good example of this is when the people of Israel were wandering in the desert for forty years. God took care of them. Their shoes and clothes never wore out. He supplied plenty of food and water for them, even though they were in the desert.

Because God considered Moses righteous, he was able to declare God's will to supply the needs of His people. If Moses had tried to rely on his own carnal abilities to feed and clothe over one million people in the desert, it would have been impossible. God agrees.

I am supposed to teach you, guide you, empower you and give you spiritual solutions to physical problems. I want to do that, but YOU choose where your help comes from: your carnal mind or me through my Spirit. Choose me.

We need to let go, and let God.

To understand more about time and eternity, read the book by Troy A. Brewer Redeeming Your Timeline[4] and listen to his DVD of the same title. These will help you understand Time and Eternity and how it's possible to redeem your timeline.

HOLINESS – Jesus had to become Messiah because humans became unholy when Adam messed up. We can understand what *unholiness* is by knowing what *holiness* is.

The Hebrew word for "holiness" is qodes, a word that highlights the realm of the sacred. The adjective qados "holy," refers to God and what belongs to Him.[5] He told me this,

Anything that doesn't belong to me is unholy.

We humans have a very narrow view about what is holy or unholy. For instance, if I would ask you to name something that's unholy, what would be your answer? Would it be sin, Satan, devil worship, murder, etc.? We never really think about things closer to home: cheating, lying, hating, gossiping, breaking a promise, not helping someone when you have a chance, not holding yourself accountable, not forgiving someone or yourself.

It's unholy to do things that Jesus wouldn't do, or to dwell on thoughts that don't come from God. We must take thoughts captive and throw them out of our minds. An example of unholy behavior is ignoring God's will.

When you are doing, saying or thinking something that Jesus wouldn't do, then it is unholy! He is the standard that God uses when He makes a judgment.

When a person makes a decision to switch to the carnal mind, worldly thinking, they've switched off the power of God's Spirit. This is what God had to say to me about that:

When my people switch to the carnal mind they put their spirits in dormant mode, (shut off from Holy Spirit). Remember that I can't commune with them there because I'm not human. When they do that, they are wading in a mire of unholiness. Do they think they won't get dirty?

My people must be clean! That's the only way people can tell them apart from the rest of the world. They must stop sloshing in the mire of unholiness (their will, not mine) and stride confidently in the cleanness of my holiness. They will not be able to be who I created them to be, to do the things I created them to do if they operate from the carnal worldly realm.

We must turn away from our unholiness so God can cleanse us, as it says in I John 1:9.

"If we confess our sins, he is faithful and just to forgive us our sins and to *cleanse us* from all unrighteousness." Italics added. God continued.

They cannot make a difference in the world until they are clean and do my will, until they are operating in my holiness.

God's messages in my latest journals mostly relate to the Church – His Ekklesia. He wants us to know that we are running out of time to make a difference in the world. He said,

Yeshua gave people ME through his righteousness. They became holy, but, if they CHOOSE to live in the carnal physical realm, they live in unholiness.

It's time to make a difference in the world, Church, my Ekklesia. It's time to be holy. Time is short!

Psalm 86:15

"But, you, O Lord, are a God merciful and gracious, slow to anger and abounding in steadfast love and faithfulness."

Father, thank You for loving us so much that You would watch Your son suffer and die a horrible death to redeem us, instead of giving us the death penalty. Jesus, I am so grateful that You chose to do the Father's will instead of your own. Help me, Lord to have a deeper relationship with you. I want to be holy and do your will. Help me, Holy Spirit, to live in my spirit instead of living from the carnal world. I praise You and thank You. Amen.

CHAPTER 2

HAVING A PERSONAL RELATIONSHIP WITH GOD

Now that we have learned a little about God, we should be able to see that God isn't that stodgy, angry, old man "upstairs" that's just waiting for us to mess up so that He can hit us with a lightning bolt or send us to hell without passing go. He actually is what humans keep looking for, but never find for themselves in the world. In addition, there is so much more that He wants you to experience with Him, more than our worldly senses can even imagine. He wants a personal relationship with you!

What We Need to Do

We can't just say we're going to have a personal relationship with God, we actually have to reach out and apply ourselves to make it happen. We became friends with God when we accepted Jesus as our Savior; now we must develop a best friend relationship. Here are things we can do to make that happen.

EXAMINE OURSELVES - Remember that God's holiness cannot exist with unholiness. We need to examine ourselves. Is there anything in our lives that is not pleasing to God, not Holy? Often times, when we give our lives to the Lord, there is something in our hearts that we just don't want to give up. There could be multiple reasons for hanging on to things that are unholy:

1. **We don't want to admit that we have a problem**. Some people grow up in a situation where they can't admit they have a problem, because that would be a sign of weakness.

2. **Through ignorance we don't know what we're holding onto is unholy.** If you never heard about God, you wouldn't even know about holiness and unholiness. Unfortunately, you may have grown up in a religious institution that doesn't teach the "hidden truths" of the Bible. That was my situation.

3. **We don't WANT to give up what we're doing.** We like it because it feels good. Or maybe it's an addiction. We tell ourselves that it's just one little thing, so no big deal.

4. **We don't like it, but it's been such a part of our lives, it's scary to think about giving it up.** At least it's familiar. Many of us are fearful about the unknown.

5. **We don't know any other way to go**. God does. Trust Him.

6. **We're just too lazy to take the time to examine ourselves.** We'd rather just watch our favorite TV show or play that video game.

7. **We're too busy to think about it.** There's meetings, and seminars, and children to take care of, bills to pay, and chores to do, school, work, sports, shopping, the list just goes on and on.

Remember, we are reaching out to have an intimate relationship with God. If we are holding something back and are not willing to take the time to give an honest examination of ourselves, how can we be honest in a relationship. He wants our whole lives, not just parts of them.

If you're not sure if something in your life is unholy, get rid of it.

If we take the time to examine ourselves and repent of anything that is unholy, then we are using discernment. Discernment describes a process of determining God's desire or identifying the true nature of things.

If we don't repent of unholy things in our lives, we can't discern the truth in those areas of our lives. (We've "switched off" the Holy Spirit's power.) We are leaving ourselves vulnerable to Satan's influence and lies. We are actually opening doors (gates) that give him an opportunity to enter into our lives.

As Christ's Church, His Ekklesia, we hold the Keys of the Kingdom. These are keys that unlock and lock the gates of hell. These gates are openings to Satan's influence and become part of His domain if we let him in.

Note: These keys were the keys of Satan's kingdom until Jesus redeemed them by defeating Satan. They are now Keys of God's Kingdom. If we have given our lives to Him, through Jesus, we are given those keys to be able to bind and release things in the spiritual realm, which then affects circumstances in the natural realm.

We should be so grateful to Jesus, that we willingly want to look for what is unholy in our lives, repent and do holy things out of our appreciation for what Jesus did. What was Jesus' desire? His desire was to exchange His righteousness for our sins and make us WHOLE and holy again.

I'm going to share a short conversation I had with Jesus.

I was using a gel pen to write in my journal. At one point I wrote the word Jesus and I accidentally smeared the word. This is our conversation:

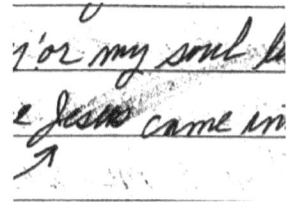

Look at how I smeared the name Jesus. Doesn't it look like it whooshed down here to be in the sentence? I think that's what you look like when you whoosh to enter someone's heart when they ask you to come in. It's like you can hardly wait to enter, and so You just whoosh in as fast as you can. Thank You, Lord!

Well, I wanted it so bad, that I sacrificed myself to a horrible torture and death on a cross to make it possible. We did everything we could to make it happen. It's up to each person now to invite me in.

Think of a thoroughbred horse race. See the horses in the gate waiting to GO when that gate opens; they're prancing and pawing and snorting. That's me waiting to GO when someone opens their heart to me. WHOOPIE!

(Laughing) Lord, you make me laugh!

Oh, my . . . that is such an astonishing demonstration of sacrificial, unconditional love.

Why do we want to keep throwing it all back in His face by holding back certain things in our lives?

HUMBLE OURSELVES - Humbleness is giving up our self-centeredness. This is very important when we want to have a intimate relationship with God. If we can't humble ourselves, then we will never be able to put our trust in God, we will not be able to give up control, even if it is harmful to us. We must put God first, because He knows what's best for us. He knows the big picture. He's told me that on several occasions.

Practice what you learn and keep trusting us. We know what's best for you, because we know the 'big picture'. And what we do and expect from you is because of our love for you.

The following are scriptures that deal with humbleness:

"Humble yourselves before the Lord, and He will lift you up." (James 4:10)

"If my people, who are called by my name, will humble themselves and pray, and seek my face and turn from their wicked ways, then I will hear from heaven and will forgive their sin and heal their land." (2 Chronicles 7:14)

"He guides the humble in what is right and teaches the humble His way." (Psalm 25:9)

We receive more grace when we humble ourselves.

"But he gives us more grace. That is why scripture says, "God opposes the proud, but shows favor to the humble."" (James 4:6)NIV

REPENT - "Repent" isn't a noun, it's a verb. That means we have to take action. It's not enough to say we repent, but we actually have to do it. Repenting means to feel regret or remorse for something then making a commitment to change for the better. In other words, we have to feel remorse over our unholy behavior or thoughts, discard them, turn away and walk in holiness. If we don't, we are risking the peace in our lives. Here are some scriptures that deal with repentance:

"Whoever conceals their sins does not prosper, but the one who confesses and renounces them finds mercy." (Proverbs 28:13)NIV

"Repent, then, and turn to God so that your sins may be wiped out, that times of refreshing may come from the Lord." (Acts 3:19)NIV

Which of us don't need refreshing in these times?

PRAY: We must pray. It's the only way to talk with God. We have a distorted view of what pray or prayer means. It's not reciting words that we've memorized, it's talking to God. Actually, there is scripture that addresses this:

"But when ye pray, use not vain repetitions . . ." (Matthew 6:7) KJV

Prayer is simply a conversation between you and God. Would you keep saying the same things over and over every time you called your friend? I think not, they'd stop answering the phone.

Prayer is two-fold: talking to God AND actually listening to God.

"Give ear, and hear my voice; give attention and hear my speech." (Isaiah 28:23)

The listening part is probably the hardest part at first, and hearing is the second hardest thing. Something God told me explained it quite well. I had asked a question and He answered it, but not until He commented on something that I had just thought to myself.

I like what you just did. You closed your eyes and said to yourself, 'Not my will but Yours, not my words but Yours.' Then you thought, 'Be still and know God.' That is so very important. There are so many distractions

29

today. People find it hard to quiet their minds so they can hear my still small voice.

People need to quiet all the noise around them, and all the clutter in their minds, which acts like 'white noise'. Nothing stops when they quiet their minds, they still need to use their minds, and I am still talking, BUT I'm not . . . I WON'T yell at them so that they can hear me above all that noise. My voice is quiet, calm, peaceful and tranquil. That's what people need in their lives.

Hmm, the trouble is when they do finally quiet their minds and all the ruckus stops, it makes them twitchy, because the silence is too big, they're not used to it. Therefore, it takes some practice to get used to the quietness.

He hit the nail on the head there. There are still times when I need to make a conscience effort to quiet my mind. But it has gotten easier and easier to hear Him and instead of the quietness being a distraction, it has become a welcoming place.

One thing that I found out is that when we first start to have that personal relationship with God, we want to do all the talking. We need to stop talking and listen occasionally. He has some very important things to tell us, but He can't do that if He can't get a word in edgewise. A friend told me that there's a reason He gave us one mouth and two ears.

I need to clarify something. When I say talk or listen to God, I don't mean an audible voice. It's a spiritual connection between His Spirit and ours, a communication you hear in your mind. I find it hard to explain, but when it happens you know it, but at first you might talk yourself out of it. I did that at first and I missed out. It wasn't until I started writing down everything I thought in my mind, that I was able to trust what I was "hearing". That's probably what you should do as well.

Luke 11:28 says, ..."**Blessed, rather, are those who hear the Word of God and keep it.**"

DO, DON'T WAIT – When God talks to you, He may tell you to do something. DO IT. One of the reasons you have this personal relationship with God is to get direction from Him. If He tells you to do something, don't sit on it, don't talk yourself out of it, just do it. That also gets easier as you go.

For instance: if God tells you to go to someone and say that He loves them, do it, because that person may need to hear that right now. Maybe they're contemplating suicide and that's the one thing they need to hear to keep them from doing it.

Remember the passage from James 2:14-17, "**What good is it, my brothers, if someone says he has faith but does not have works? Can that faith save him? So also faith by itself, if it does not have works, is dead.**"

If you have faith that God loves a person, what good is it if you don't do anything to let that person know? We can't just sit back and do nothing. We must listen to what God is telling us to do and then go do it.

That reminds me of something that happened with my dad. Dad is 91 years old. In 2016 he fell out of my semi-tractor and had a MAJOR head trauma. The doctors knew he wouldn't live. But God had a different idea about that. Dad was in a coma for forty three days and in rehab for six months.

Almost a year later Dad has a stroke. The doctors knew he wouldn't live. But God had a different idea about that. My dad has recovered from the stroke, but he does get confused and his memory is not what it was. Plus, he has Fugh's Dystrophy and his eyesight is getting worse and worse, so he gets discouraged sometimes. He can't do a lot of the things he used to do and sometimes he feels worthless.

In 2018, Dad and I went to a Collingsworth Family[6] concert and after the concert we were in line to talk to Kim, the mother. While we were waiting our turn, a man came up to Dad, put his hand on Dad's shoulder and said, "You don't know me, and I don't know you, but I'm supposed to tell you that God is not done with you yet." He then turned and walked away.

Wow, you can imagine how encouraging those words can be to Dad when he's feeling low and worthless. God still needs him. What if that man had not done what God told him to do . . .?

ADDENDUM: I was going to rewrite this page, using the past tense, but I've decided just to add this comment. My Dad passed away on July 22, 2022. He was 91 years old.

Because He knew that God was not done with him yet, he was able to witness to others, through his singing, for another two and a half years. God needed him. God needs all of us, young or old.

James 4:17

"So whoever knows the right thing to do and fails to do it, for him it is sin."

Thank You Lord, for Your salvation. That is a priceless gift. I can't pay You back, but I can try my best to do the works that You have ordained for me, so that others can believe in You and be saved. I give You honor and praise and glory. Amen.

What God Will Do

A relationship is a two-party activity. There are certain things that God will do when you have a personal relationship with Him.

HE WILL LET YOU KNOW HOW MUCH HE LOVES YOU AND CARES FOR YOU - He'll keep reminding you of that. Here are some examples of what He's told me over the last year:

We love you! You are a treasure to us.

We encircle you with our love.

I am proud of you. You are precious to me, and I want to spend more and more time with you.

We so look forward to our conversations. They are so precious to us. We love you so much.

Not only will He tell you He loves you, but He'll also show you that He loves and cares for you on a personal basis. One of the most astonishing examples of this happened when I was singing with *The Guardian Quartet* from Ohio.

> We were singing at a rest home and everyone was gathered in the Great Room to hear us; everyone except one woman who didn't want to come into the room. She stayed in the hallway on a recliner, but she could still hear our concert. After our last song, Kay, our soprano, told our accompanist, Ginny, to give us the notes to the song we had just finished and we would sing it a cappella to the woman in the hall.
>
> Ginny said, "It's gone." I asked, "What's gone?" She told me the sheet music was gone, it wasn't on the piano where she'd left it. People were walking out of the

room, so we figured that the music had blown off the piano, but we couldn't find it anywhere.

Kay finally said to Ginny to find another song that we could do a cappella, and Ginny flipped through our notebook and said, "Here's one you can do a cappella, "He Touched Me." So she gave us the notes and we went and sang to the woman.

By the time we were done, the woman was in tears. She thanked us and said how much she appreciated our song. She told us that she had just lost her husband a little over a week ago, and was feeling so sad, that she had asked God to help her cope because she missed her husband so much.

She said, "Thank you so much, you have no idea how much you've done for me." Then she said something that gave me goose bumps, "That was my husband's favorite song." Wow.

We finally went back into the Great Room to pack up and there on the piano was the music for the last song we had sung for our concert, right where Ginny had left it. It was always there, we just couldn't see it because God knew that the woman needed to hear "He Touched Me".

When God says He wants a PERSONAL relationship, He means it.

He tells us in Isaiah 41:13, **"For I, the Lord your God, hold your right hand; it is I who say, "Fear not, I am the one who helps you."**

HE WILL TEACH YOU – Psalm 32:8 mentions, **"I will instruct you and teach you in the way you should go; I will counsel you with my eye upon you."**

One of my most appreciated things that God has done for me, is to teach me the hidden truths of the Bible. In our modern church these truths have been neglected or watered down.

As I said in the Introduction, there are so many of His people that just don't understand these basic truths. That is so sad. These truths help us to understand who we are in Christ and what we need to do to be who we were created to be and do the things we were created to do. They will help us to be a good disciple of God. This is what He told me,

I'm happy to show you my Truth, because it will set you free to soar, to shine and to live to your fullest potential.

God is not happy with the leadership of His Church and one of the reasons is because they are not teaching His Truths.

HE WILL TRAIN YOU – God won't just tell you what He wants you to accomplish, He will train you to do it. That is very important, and is explained in 2 Timothy 3:16.

"All scripture is breathed out by God and profitable for teaching, for reproof, for correction, and for training in righteousness."

God will also train us through Jesus' example and by the lives of others, through videos, books and live action. He will also have you practice what you are learning. I must admit, that's a little scary. I'm still working on trusting what He's showing me, and though I'm still somewhat anxious, I won't give up.

The hardest part about practicing is learning to let go of our what-ifs: what if they don't want to talk, what if I can't do it, what if it makes the person uncomfortable or mad, what if I mess it up, what if they laugh at me, what if that person doesn't believe in God, yada, yada, yada.

It seems we can find many excuses not to do what He's telling us to do. At some point, we're just going to have to do it. Otherwise, we won't be doing God's will, and that's not a good thing. Practice allows us to gain confidence, which gives us the boldness we need to be effective.

When you are learning a skill, you don't just go out and do it. You have to learn it step-by-step and then practice each step as you go. Eventually, you will become proficient and people will seek your services. It's the same way here.

So, just let go and do, even though your heart is pounding and you feel like you're gonna throw up. At first it may be slow-going, but as you gain confidence, you will have more and more success, until people are seeking your service.

I have gone up to people and asked if I could pray for them, and all but one said yes. Even if there seemed to be no change in their circumstances at the time, they appreciated the fact that someone cared enough about them to pray for them. Don't assume that there wasn't a change; it may take a day or so.

There have been a few times where there has been manifested results. What I mean is that it's already a done deal in heaven, and was called forth and became real in the physical realm.

Training is great, and the greatest thing about having a trainer is that they know what to show you because they've already had experience. Eventually you will be able to do what they themselves have done.

Luke 6:40 explains this, **"A disciple is not above His teacher, but everyone, when he is fully trained, will be like his teacher."**

Therefore, it is with us. We will be able to do all that God can do. That is awesome!

Eventually, we will become the trainer, as God's representatives, and teach a new generation of believers.

God has told me that He has accelerated training; as a result His blessings are manifesting faster and faster all over the world. We are going into a worldwide revival.

One last thing about training you need to know: God also uses discipline to train us, even though we don't appreciate it sometimes.

Hebrews 12:11 teaches us, **"For the moment, all discipline seems painful rather than pleasant, but later it yields the peaceful fruit of righteousness."**

HE WILL GIVE SPIRITUAL SOLUTIONS – Proverbs 3:5-6 says, **"Trust in the Lord with all your heart, and do not lean on your own understanding. In all your ways acknowledge Him, and He will make straight your paths."**

When we are suffering or have a problem that seems hopeless, we will try anything to find relief. As carnal humans, in our carnal minds we think we have to find carnal solutions to our carnal problems. However, if we are children of God, then we live from His presence through Holy Spirit. He can find spiritual solutions to our worldly situations. This is what He told me:

You are a spiritual being and you need to operate from the spiritual realm. Your spirit in mine has authority over this world and anything that occurs.

Every physical, human problem has a spiritual solution as well as a physical solution. However, physical ones are usually temporary and aren't necessarily what's best for you. The spiritual solutions I give you are everlasting. Why? They are divine and come from heaven, and they are being done on earth as it is in heaven.

Spiritual solutions come from the Holy Spirit and are often times unexpected. I had a personal experience with this.

> I once worked for a van company. As I was driving down the freeway, the bottom mirror on my right side dual mirror fell out of the bracket. It was dangling by the heater wires.
>
> I pulled over to the side of the road and slowed to stop, but then I thought that another spot up the road by an entrance ramp would be better. However, I was in an ok spot, so I braked to stop, and again I had the thought to go further up to the side of the entrance ramp. I finally shrugged my shoulders, pulled up there, and parked. It really was safer there.
>
> I looked around in the van but I could not find anything to secure the mirror in the bracket, no rope, no tape, nothing. I didn't even have anything to cut the wires. So I got out of the van to see if I could break the wires somehow to take the mirror off.
>
> I walked around the front of the vehicle to the passenger side and stood facing the mirror. I was debating with myself on what to do when I looked down at my foot and there was a thin, rubber strap laying there.

Neat. I picked up the strap, was able to put the mirror back in the bracket, and tied it in place with the strap. The mirror stayed in place until I got back to the office.

Cutting the wires would have been a physical solution to the physical problem of the dangling mirror. However, that would have created another physical problem, which would need to be addressed. Holy Spirit's solution allowed me to keep using the mirror, which was safer than not having it, and didn't create an additional problem to deal with. Spiritual solutions are best.

The road I was driving on was I-77 in Ohio, and it is 163 miles long. What's the chance that I would pull over and stop at the exact place where there was a solution to my problem? If I had stopped where I originally wanted to, I would never have found the strap.

It was not a coincident, folks, it was a spiritual solution to my physical problem. Had I not payed attention to that . . . feeling that I should pull up and stop where I did, I would not have been able to fix the problem. I know that "feeling" was the Holy Spirit nudging me.

When you have a problem, ask the Lord to help you. That's what I did when the mirror fell out. I simply said, "Help me, Lord". And He did. Don't forget to pay attention to any nudging the Holy Spirit may be doing.

HE WILL EMPOWER YOU – When you became a child of God, you received His authority through Jesus. This empowers you to act in the Lord's name.

"There is none like You, O Lord; You are great and your name is great in might." As said in Jeremiah 10:6.

God has put all authority under Jesus; His name is above all names. Why? He sits at the right hand of God who has given Him authority over everything under His feet. This includes the world and the second heaven where Satan and his minions are.

Ephesians 1:22 KJV says, **"and hath put all things under His feet, and gave Him to be the head over all things to the Church, which is his body . . ."**

Remember that we represent Him through the authority He has given to us. We are acting in His name, under His authority.

John 14:13 states this, "**Whatever you ask in my name** [under His authority], **this I will do, that the father may be glorified in the Son."** (Bracketed words added)

If we are acting under the Lord's authority, He will grant us anything we ask, according to God's will.

We must have faith, though. Often times, we don't look at a situation from the right point-of-view and that can hinder the Holy Spirit's power.

"For my thoughts are not your thoughts, neither are your ways my ways, saith the Lord. For as the heavens are higher than the earth, so are my ways higher than your ways, and my thoughts than your thoughts." (Isaiah 55:8-9) KJV

I'll tell you about a vision I had. In my vision I was looking out at the world from a mouth of an underground cave. I asked God what that was all about and this is what He told me:

Don't look at things from below the ground looking up, but from your true point-of-view: from heaven looking down. Remember, you are here with us; we are one. So our point-of-view is also your point-of-view.

Unfortunately, that is another problem with God's Church. We're looking at things from the wrong perspective. Either we were never taught this, or we've forgotten that God's perspective should also be our perspective. If it isn't, then we are looking at it from the world's perspective, we're looking at it with our carnal minds. We've hindered the Holy Spirit because our "switch" is in the OFF position. Our spirits are dormant, temporarily inactive, so to speak.

HE WILL GIVE YOU POWER – Acts 1:8 says, **"But you will receive power when the Holy Spirit has come upon you."**

When we gave our lives to the Lord we received His Holy Spirit, and He gave us the faith we need to believe. Then when we activate our spirits by flipping the switch ON, we receive power from Holy Spirit to do God's will. The Oxford Languages' definition of power is:

1. **The ability to do something or act in a particular way,**

2. **The capacity or ability to direct or influence the behavior of others or the course of events.**[7]

The Holy Spirit's power gives us the ability to do things that would be impossible if we relied on our own carnal power. Here's an example:

> My son and daughter were involved in a crash, and the side of the van was caved in. My son, who had been in the front, could not get to my daughter. She was unconscious in the twisted back end of the van.
>
> My son jumped out of the front, ran to the back of the van, and jerked the doors open to get to my daughter. Later, a firefighter commented that they would have had to use the jaws-of-life to get the doors open, it would have been impossible without it. **NOTHING is impossible with God!**

As soon as I was notified about the crash I called as many prayer chains as I could think of. My daughter was taken to the Children's Hospital. She was only a few weeks away from being too old to go there. My husband and I picked up my son who was at the crash site and drove to the hospital. We couldn't see our daughter at first, because they were working to stabilize her.

Finally, a doctor came out and told us that my daughter had the most damaged, broken spleen he had ever seen, and that they needed to operate to remove it. However, they had to wait at least three days, until she was more stable.

(I want to add a side comment here. Prior to the accident, my kids were at each other's throats. There wasn't a day that went by that they weren't yelling at each other. This went on for months and to this day, I don't know why they were so angry with each other.)

The doctor let us go see my daughter in the triage room before they took her to intensive care, even though she was unconscious. Her blond hair was red from blood because she had a head injury, and there were tubes coming out of her body everywhere. My son, who had been driving the van, was shaking and barely able to hold back tears. I was trying to hold it together for everybody else.

All of a sudden, my daughter's eyes fluttered open and she barely raised her hand and in a very weak voice said my son's name. He went over to the bed and held her hand. Then I heard her small, weak voice say, "It's ok. I still love you." And my son just started sobbing. Well, that did it for me and my husband, we both started sobbing, too.

You know, I never heard my kids fight after that. They realized that their first thoughts after the accident were of each other.

In this book you've seen messages from God that tell us how much He loves us and wants to take care of us. He means that when He says it in Nahum 1:7,

"The Lord is good, a stronghold in the day of trouble; he knows those who take refuge in him."

So now the rest of the story:

The person inside the SUV that had broadsided the van was not injured, and so she ran to the back of the van to attend to my daughter. *She was a medical doctor!*

The SUV hit the van in the only place it could have to keep the van from completely collapsing and crushing my daughter, the support beams for a hydraulic lift that had been installed for my disabled sister-in-law.

When the SUV hit the van, it pushed the van into another vehicle, which kept it from rolling over.

And the most miraculous of them all, my daughter's worst damaged spleen ever, healed within days, so they never did the operation. Her head injury only needed six stitches to close.

What an awesome God we serve! And God bless all the people that prayed for my kids.

Another aspect of "power" is the ability to influence the course of events.

> Years ago, I lived at a camp with my family. My husband and I were caretakers there. We were getting the camp ready for a minister's group that was coming for the weekend. It had rained for a few days and the grass was very high. I was mowing an area that desperately needed mowed.
>
> Large, very dark clouds started rolling in and the wind started blowing very hard. Two raindrops hit me. I told the Lord that He needed to help me. If He wanted the place to look nice for the group when they arrived, He was going to have to, please, stop the rain from coming. I didn't feel any more raindrops after that, and we were able to finish preparing the camp. It never did rain anymore even though it was very dark and windy.
>
> Later, as I was watching the local news I found out that there had been severe rain caused by two tornadoes that went through the area, one of which was only a half mile away. The next day I talked to some neighbors and they commented about how bad the rain had been. Huh. Apparently, the only place it didn't rain was on the camp property.

Wow, what an awesome God we serve!

Prayer and faith: two of the most powerful ways we have of releasing the Holy Spirit's power. These are benefits of having a personal relationship with God.

We need an intimate relationship with God so that He can show us the Truth, the truth that sets us free, as it says in John 8:32.

"And you will know the truth, and the truth will set you free."

There is a message that God has for you:

Step out in faith and keep asserting my Truth. My Truth is what sets people free, especially my own people who are bound. If my people don't LIVE my Truth, they are saved, but NOT free. They don't belong to Satan, but they are still bound. I've given them the keys to unlock their shackles, but they won't unlock them. Why? They're using their carnal minds, not their spirits to find solutions for the world's problems.

If we are to make a difference in the world, we have to have that personal relationship with God so that the Holy Spirit can give us the solutions and power that we need to unlock our shackles and set ourselves, and others, free.

John 14:26 says that the Holy Spirit is our helper, " **But the helper, the Holy Spirit, whom the Father will send in my name, He will teach You all things and bring to your remembrance all that I have said to you."**

This is what I told Jesus once,

Thank You for making it possible for me to open my heart to You, and of course, for You rushing in. He responded:

It's my absolute pleasure! I so love people. Oh how I long for every single person to invite me into their hearts.

Ephesians 3:16

"For this reason I bow my knees to the Father, that according to the riches of His glory, He may grant you to be strengthened with power through His Spirit in your inner being."

Dear Father,

I am amazed at your wondrous power, and how much you love and care for each of us. Holy Spirit, please help me to grab hold of Father's blessings, trust Him and take the power you have for me and make a difference in other people's lives. In Jesus' name I pray.

Ways We Can Learn to Commune with God

Since having a personal relationship with God is not something that's talked about in our churches, it's difficult for us to know how to commune with Him. It's been a struggle, but I'm finally getting the hang of it.

SPEND TIME WITH GOD – One thing that really helped me was setting a particular time of day to sit down and be still and know Him. For me, that time is early in the morning just after the sun rises. That's usually the time I get up in the mornings.

Whatever time you chose, try making it a daily thing. You want it to become a part of your daily routine. It will eventually be something that you'll look forward to.

I Chronicles 16:11 tells us to seek God all the time. **"Seek the Lord and His strength; seek His presence continually!"**

Don't become too busy to spend time with God. You need that time to develop a relationship with Him. This is what He told me about that.

People need to know me. I'm not talking about knowing facts about me; most of my people know quite a bit about me. What I'm talking about is 'knowing' as having an intimate relationship with me. It's like any other close relationship in people's lives.

46

Your best friends are best friends because you know them; the likes and dislikes, dreams and goals, what makes them happy or sad, what pleases them or makes them angry or upset. You know that your best friends can be trusted, because they have never forsaken you, have always been there through thick and thin. Well, I will never forsake you and I will always be there for you, but you have to get to know me before you can trust that what I'm saying is true.

LET THE WORLD GO – The lives we lived before we were saved, were all about worldly things. It's hard to let go of things that have always been a part of our lives.

I John 2:15-17 says that we have to let go of the worldly things. "**Do not love the world or the things in the world. If anyone loves the world, the love of the Father is not in him. For all that is in the world – the desires of the flesh and the desires of the eyes and pride in life – is not from the Father but is from the world. And the world is passing away along with its desires, but whoever does the will of God abides forever.**"

Remember, it was the desire of the flesh, desire of the eyes and pride of life that was the downfall of Adam and Eve.

We must learn to let go of the worldly things and put God first. If we seek Him, He will take care of us. He has many blessings He wants to give us. If we want to connect with God, we must put all the worldly things out of our minds so we can hear His quiet voice.

Take some deep breaths through your nose and let them out slowly through your mouth. Deep breathing helps lower stress levels and calm you down. It also helps you focus. You need to close your eyes and envision yourself sitting calmly.

Try to let go of the concerns, problems and thoughts of the world. When your mind starts to wander, make a conscious effort to refocus your mind on spiritual things. Say, "Not my will, but yours." Each time you take authority over carnal thoughts, you'll find that you're needing to do it less and less. Learning to switch from the carnal mind to spiritual mind is not easy; it actually can be quite frustrating. I had a vision that pertained to this topic:

> I was underneath some sort of blocks that were hovering above me. They were like heavy balloon blocks, except you couldn't break them. I had to get through them to get out from under them. I started pushing on them and they would move some but they wanted to slip back in place. So I started punching them quickly so that they couldn't float back in place. Eventually, I was able to squeeze my upper body through. I kept pushing and punching, seeming like I would never get through. Then at last I was able to get my whole body through. I knew this was some sort of message for me, so I asked God what it meant. The Holy Spirit replied:

> *Of course the blocks represent the things that are blocking you from achieving the ability to completely free your spiritual senses. It's an ongoing struggle, and when you've cleared enough space to squeeze through, the block floats back to fill a part of that space and you have to punch some more. But each time you are able to squeeze through further. You keep punching away until you are finally able to break through.*

> *This is what you are going through right now. It represents your struggle, but it also shows you that if you keep punching away, you will succeed.*

Learning to use your true senses is difficult, because the world has separated the spiritual entity from the carnal entity, and focused all the attention on the carnal. Many people now don't even realize that they are spiritual beings, let alone that their true identity is through their spirits. Jesus came to bring us back to wholeness.

PRAISE AND WORSHIP GOD – Once you feel calm and you've let go of the worldly stuff then begin to praise and worship God. It could be as simple as thinking of how He's blessed you and thanking Him for that. Tell Him how His blessings have helped you or changed something for the better, or thank Him for people in your life that He has sent your way to help you. Praise Him for His creation. I usually sit outside, so that is easy for me to do; I just look around and thank Him for what I see or hear.

You could sing or play a song. Music is a great way to get into the right frame of mind. Pick a song that speaks to your heart, and it will speak to His as well. Remember, you are one. Focus on heavenly things, as it says in Colossians 3:2.

"Set your minds on things that are above, not on things that are on the earth."

ASK THE HOLY SPIRIT FOR HELP – Ask Him to guide you and to help you hear God's voice. Thank Him for always being there and helping you, and teaching you, etc.

One thing I've learned while writing this book, is that the Holy Spirit is more than willing to help us when we ask. Without His direction, I could not have written this book, amen and halleluiah!

You need to put your trust in Holy Spirit and He will give you the knowledge, wisdom, strength and power to do what needs to done. Learn this Truth from Philippians 4:13 and declare it. **"I can do all things through Him who strengthens me."**

KEEP A JOURNAL – Keeping a journal is one of the best things you can do. It really helps you to focus and keep your mind on God.

I highly recommend it. After I started journaling, I became less distracted and more focused. Don't over think, just start writing.

Write down your thoughts, questions, etc. then give Him time to respond. Write down what you hear in your mind. If you're not sure where the words are coming from, ask Him if they're your words or His. He'll let you know. Separate your words from His by using different fonts or italics, etc.

When I write in my journals, I use cursive for my words and printing for His. There are some days I don't journal, but I still spend a little time each day to say hi in the morning and at the end of each day I'll thank Him for being with me and tell Him good night. I'll also speak to Him during the day.

When I finally decided to journal, I knew it was going to be a while before I "heard" anything from Him, because I didn't know what I was doing. The following is my very first journal entry.

Tuesday November 26, 2019

It's so encouraging to read Matthew's book about his conversations with you.[8] Thank You for speaking to us today. Thank You for revealing Your heart. I give You mine. What does that mean to you?

I decided to ask a question because someone said it was good to do to see if He would answer. I waited, not really expecting an answer, but, all of a sudden, these words came to me,

It means being still and knowing that I am God. It's knowing that I love you no matter what you do or don't do. I want the best for you, because I created you out of my love for you. I want to shower you with blessings. I want to guide you in every aspect of your life, for I know the life I ordained for you.

50

I believe it was at this point I was thinking something like the fact that I wasn't worthy for all this, then He spoke again.

> *You are worthy because you are my child! And I'm such a proud father! Now, you giving me your heart also means this to me: Show others my heart through yours. I will be with you always, and nothing is impossible with me. Shalom.*

I was so surprised that He actually responded on my very first entry. I even asked the Holy Spirit if they were my words or His. He assured me they were His. He spoke to me again on my fifth entry. Now, it's usually not more than one or two days before He communicates with me . . . little old me. . .

In my latest journals God has given me messages that can be three to six pages long, but that's because He has important messages for His Church for this time we are in. I will reveal them in this book. Actually, the messages are the main reason He had me write this book.

God wants people to write things down so that others can read and know the Truth, the things now and things that He wants us to know about the future. Revelation 1:19 reveals this.

"Write therefore the things that you have seen, those that are and those that are to take place after this."

Not only has God given me messages through His words, but also through visions. Visions help people understand a concept better because we have a "picture" of what the message means. Habakkuk 2:2 explains that we should write down our vision as well.

"Write the vision; make it plain on tablets, so he may run who reads it."

I had a vision where I was in heaven and sitting with Father God. Here is our conversation.

> *Welcome. I have so much to show you. I'm glad you have chosen to come here. It makes me very happy. You've been here before, remember?*

> Yes. I was sitting here with you and we were looking down at the people on earth and You told me that You wanted all of them to be a part of Your kingdom; that You love each of them as much as You love Your Son, Jesus.

> That's right. And you can come sit with me anytime you want.

God will use multiple ways of getting His message across to us. When we write things down it gives us the chance to reread the messages to encourage us, remind us of something, and so we have a way of telling others about God and His love, as I am doing with this book. This is one of our purposes that He has ordained.

USE YOUR IMAGINATION – When God made us in His image, imagination was one of the things that was included. We need to activate our imaginations to be able to see in the spiritual realm. God uses it to communicate with us. He told me that it's very important for us to use our imaginations, and was upset that we adults think imagination is childish. Here's what He had to say:

We created humans in our image and imagination is part of that. In fact, most of the inventions on earth happened in heaven first and implanted into someone's imagination. Unfortunately, many of my people think imagination is childish and it should be ignored.

Did I not say that to enter my kingdom you must become like a child? Children are humble, but they have powerful imaginations, and they are not afraid to use them. That is why it is much easier for children to believe in me. They haven't squelched their imaginations and limited my Spirit.

The key is to have the mind of Yeshua. He was not afraid to use his imagination. His creative miracles came from his imagination, which is MY imagination. We are interconnected, so your imaginations are mine as well, through Yeshua.

If someone is not interconnected with me, then their imagination can be polluted by Satan. A person's imagination is part of their being, so Satan can influence it if a person is not connected to me, and empowered by the Holy Spirit. That's what happened at the Tower of Babel. Read Genesis 11:1-9. That's why the key is to have the mind of Yeshua.

God created the universe using His imagination. He envisioned it then spoke it into existence through Jesus and the Holy Spirit's power made it happen. We must do the same.

Unfortunately, some people have fallen for Satan's lies and have misused their imaginations. This is what God had to say,

I gave my imagination to humans. Whatever they can imagine they can create. Unfortunately, some use it to create evil things . I create wonderful, good things and it grieves my heart when they are used to cause grief and pain.

When someone misuses God's gift, and trauma and tragedy happens because of it, and everything seems hopeless, God still loves that person.

But I will never shut off my love for anyone. Besides, nothing is hopeless. The circumstances can still be made right, because in my spiritual realm there is a solution, a cure, a resolution. The problem is that humankind has forgotten that. With us all things are possible.

It's through your imagination that visions, songs, poems, drawings, solutions, inventions, etc. come from. You must activate your imagination to receive what God wants to give you.

There is so much that God wants to bless us with, and He gave us Holy Spirit to teach us, show us Jesus, and He gives us His gifts to empower us to do what we've been ordained to do.

I Corinthians 12:7-10 lists some of those gifts. **Wisdom, understanding, faith, healing, miracles, prophesy, discerning of spirits, tongues, and interpreting of tongues.**

In Romans 12:5-7 other gifts are mentioned. **Service, teaching, exhortation, generosity, diligence, mercy.**

More gifts from Holy Spirit are mentioned in Ephesians 4:11. **Apostles, evangelists, and pastors.**

I Peter 4:10 says what we are to do with these gifts: "**As each has received a gift, use it to serve one another, as good stewards of God's varied grace.**" This is part of our commission.

All of these are important to God's disciples and Holy Spirit gives them to us as needed, as stated in I Corinthians 12:11.

"All these are empowered by one and the same Spirit, who apportions each one individually as He wills."

One day I closed my eyes to get into "My time with God" mode, and suddenly I saw a drawing. A few days later, I received the makings of a poem. I realized that they went together, so I wrote them down. (See the next page.)

I AM SET FREE

Almighty God, can you hear me?
My life is such a mess!
If You are real, I'm reaching out,
Because I'm in distress.

You pick me up and brush me off
And wrap your arms around me.
You whisper, "It will be ok,
Because I set you free."

"I'm Father's Son who bore your sins;
Paid the cost that should be yours."
Oh, Mighty God, I'm not worthy!
And I collapse upon the floor.

You pick me up and once again
You wrap your arms around me.
You whisper, "It will be ok'
Because I set you free."

Well then,

I praise and worship You and Him,
Almighty God, my Father!
I fell again; You love me still.
I'm amazed You even bother.

And once again, You pick me up
And wrap Your arms around me.
"Oh my dear child, it's okay.
Remember, you are free!"

- Patricia S Welsh
© December 2019

Whatever your talents or your abilities, whether art, music, cooking, woodworking, sewing, speaking, writing, community service, sports, preaching, serving, etc., God will give ideas and direction through your imagination. Don't squelch it, because you are limiting the Holy Spirit when you do. Remember, God wants you to soar!

PRAY UNCEASINGLY – Your special quiet time with God is only a small part of your day. Don't ignore Him the rest of the day. Remember, He's always with us. I Thessalonians 5:16-18 says,

"Rejoice always, pray without ceasing, give thanks in all circumstances; for this is the will of God in Christ Jesus for you."

At first, praying without ceasing seems impossible. However, remember that praying is just talking with God.

When you have a relationship with someone and are together, you don't ignore that person all day; at least you shouldn't! You communicate throughout the day – *"Thanks for bringing me coffee." "Did you hear what happened at the market yesterday?" "I love you." "Let's go for a drive." "Did I ever tell you how much I appreciate you?"*

You also communicate your love and care for each other just by your presence and attention without saying a word. This is what your relationship with God should be.

I remember one time I had an open vision when I was sitting in a patio chair on the side porch during my quiet time with God. An open vision is a vision, but you can look and see the physical things around you. I was drinking coffee. I looked at another patio chair and I had a sense of someone sitting there. I realized it was Jesus and He was sipping a cup of coffee. He looked at me and smiled. We just sat there enjoying the morning and each other's company.

To this day I can still picture that, and it's as precious to me now as it was then.

Speak to God throughout your day – *"Ooo, that was a beautiful bird, thanks for creating it." "I love You." "Please help me find my car keys." "It makes me so sad when people are fighting; I can't imagine how that makes You feel." "Did You hear what happened at the market yesterday?" "Thanks for helping me find my keys." "Did I ever tell You how much I appreciate You?"*

It takes practice to pray unceasingly, but as you come to know God and your relationship with Him, it will become easier to be aware of His presence throughout the day. We had a conversation about this.

> *It takes faith, because your carnal mind still wants to operate in the physical realm. You must have faith in what Yeshua accomplished and you must have faith in me.*

> I notice the more I let the things of this world affect me, the less I'm able to hear Your voice; the harder it is for me to experience You.

> *Yes, that's why you must pray unceasingly and take authority over the things of the world. The more you do that, the easier it becomes.*

He told me something that helped me understand what praying unceasingly is. He said it's like talking to your friend on the phone while you are doing something at home.

REREAD YOUR JOURNALS – When I reread my journal the first time, I was amazed how many topics we had covered. I was also amazed at how many times God had spoken to me. It reinforced just how much He loves and cares for me.

Whenever you feel discouraged, sad, lonely, unproductive, angry, confused or even glad, reread your journal. It will pick you up and make you feel that there is hope, and that there really is nothing impossible with God.

Psalm 37:4

"Delight yourself in the Lord, and He will give you the desires of your heart."

Dear Lord,

You are such an amazing God. You do everything You can to help us have a personal relationship with You. You never give up on us, and I appreciate that. I'm going to try my very best to stay in contact with You throughout my day. Thank You so much.

CHAPTER 3

NOW WHAT?

Now that we have a personal relationship with God, what now?

Never Abandon the Relationship

Your relationship with God is the most valuable thing in your life.

IT'S YOUR CONNECTION TO GOD'S PROMISES – The Bible is filled with God's promises concerning His benefits;

1. **Deliverance:** *"When the righteous cry out for help, the Lord hears and delivers them; out of all their trouble."* (Psalm 34:17)

2. **Desires:** *"Delight yourself in the Lord, and He will give you the desires of your heart.* (Psalm 37:4)

3. *Direction:* *"For I know the plans I have for you, declares the Lord, plans for welfare and not for evil, to give you a future and a hope."* (Jeremiah 29:11)

4. **Freedom:** *"So if the Son sets you free, you will be free indeed."* (John 8:36)

5. **Friendship:** *"No longer do I call you servants, for the servant does not know what the master is doing, but I have called you friends . . ."* (John 15:15)

6. **Health:** *"By his (Jesus) wounds you have been healed."* (I Peter 2:24)

7. **Instruction:** *"I will instruct you and teach you in the way you should go."* (Psalm 32:8)

8. **Joy:** *"Those who sow in tears shall reap with shouts of joy!"* (Psalm 126:5)

9. **Peace:** *"And the peace of God, which surpasses all understanding, will guard your hearts and your minds in Christ Jesus."* (Philippians 4:7-9)

10. **Protection:** *"The Lord will fight for you; and you have only to be silent."* (Exodus 14:14)

11. **Provision:** *"And my God will supply every need according to His riches in His glory in Christ Jesus."* (Philippians 4:19)

12. **Refuge:** *"The Lord is a [refuge] for the oppressed, a stronghold in times of trouble.* (Psalm 9:9) NIV

13. **Rest:** *"Come to me, all who labor and are heavy laden, and I will give you rest."* (Matthew 11:28-29)

14. **Strength:** *"Fear not, for I am with you; be not dismayed, for I am your God; I will strengthen you, I will help you.* (Isaiah 41:10)

15. **Vigor, Energy:** *"But they who wait for the Lord . . . shall run and not be weary, they shall walk and not be faint.* (Isaiah 40:31)

When you let the worldly things take precedence in your life, when you start living from your carnal mind, you risk losing the benefits of His promises. How many times, though, do we let that happen in the course of our lives?

If you look at all these benefits, and there's even more, we notice something astonishing: the things that we are risking ARE THE VERY THINGS THAT HUMANS YEARN AND SEEK FOR THEIR ENTIRE LIVES!

Isn't that incredible? They very things that we spend a lifetime searching for, and promised to us by our Creator, we're willing to give up . . . for what? The things we DO NOT want in our lives: confusion, fear, bondage, oppression, chaos, sickness, pain, despair, hate, sin, unhappiness, depression, hunger, heartache, sadness, betrayal . . . We humans can be thickheaded sometimes.

YOU ARE VUNERABLE – When a child of God switches over to the carnal mind, that person turns off the power from God's Spirit. At that point they are leaving themselves vulnerable to Satan.

Because Adam blew it back in the Garden of Eden, Satan is the god of this world. He is the ruler of the carnal realm, because Adam essentially handed over his authority to Satan when he decided to do what Satan wanted instead of what God wanted.

God created the earth, a beautiful, bountiful place, but because of sin it's been polluted. God told me this,

I created earth to function a certain way, a place where humans could enjoy my creation and still have a personal relationship with me. And we did, until Adam and Eve rejected me. As a result, because of Satan's influence, the earth has become something it was never intended to be.

It's not my will that there is fear, doubt, pain, drought, famine, hate, slavery, confusion, hopelessness, greed, death, hunger, the list goes on and on. Evil is NOT my will.

Yes, by my will I gave humans authority over the earth, but it was never my will that they abuse that authority. Because of Satan's influence, they use it to pollute the world; I don't just mean physically, but spiritually as

well. They have taken things that were holy (mine) and polluted them; they have made them unholy; not of me, not mine.

"Be sober minded, be watchful. Your adversary the devil prowls around like a roaring lion, seeking someone to devour." So says 1 Peter 5:8.

When we switch to our carnal mind, we've shut off our power; our radar, our defense system, and the light of Jesus. In one of our conversations, God said the following,

Remember, I am spirit and can't commune with you through your carnal mind. Unfortunately, most of my Church is trying to live through their earthly senses. This causes three major problems:

1. *They can't commune with me and know my will.*

2. *They leave themselves open to the lies of Satan and that leaves them very vulnerable.*

3. *They can't do what I need them to do and be who I created them to be.*

As a result, my will is not being done, and the condition of the world reflects that.

GOD'S WILL CAN'T BE DONE – When we try and live through our carnal minds we can't do God's will. There is no way that we can change the world if we aren't switched on to our power source. The only way to accomplish the kind of change that the world needs is through the Creator Himself. We need to be empowered by Him to use His authority to change the world. That can only happen if we have a spiritual power connection with Him.

God's will is that everything would conform to His original divine plan. Everything He created was perfect, everything in balance.

Then Satan decided he wanted to be top dog and revolted against God. He lost. Now, because of jealousy, he is in the world trying to destroy God's goodness. He wants everything to be the opposite of what God wants. As a result, the world is in upheaval. His biggest target is YOU, God's people. So quit messing around, and turn the switch back on! Get your protection and power back now!

Matthew 26:41

"Watch and pray that you may not enter into temptation. The spirit indeed is willing, but the flesh is weak."

Help me Lord to stay turned on to you. I am weak, but You are strong. I know that You will give me the power to stand firm with You if I keep my mind focused on You and not on worldly things. Help me Holy Spirit. Amen.

Do God's Will

One of the major reasons for a personal relationship with God is to know His will. Everything starts there. This is what God told me,

My will is why things exist. It's why natural and spiritual laws exists. It's why all my blessings exist. It is why I sent my Son to earth as a redeemer, for it's my will that everyone be saved. It's my will that I have a personal relationship with each person. It's my will that people help each other, by passing my love on to others.

Doing God's will is the purpose of our lives. **"But for this purpose I have raised you up, to show you my power, so that my name may be proclaimed in all the earth."** This is Exodus 9:16

Our purpose is to spread God's love so that his name is proclaimed all over the world. We can do that because He gives us His *supernatural* power, which we receive through the Holy Spirit. It's through the relationship we've built with Him that the Holy Spirit can move His power and light through us into the world.

WE HAVE BEEN PREDESTINED – Before we were conceived, our purpose was written. God talked to me about this.

Every person conceived has a purpose, including you, and I have written a book that contains everything about your life that I have purposed for you.

Every single person has a predestined purpose. IT'S NO ACCIDENT THAT YOU WERE BORN; I don't care what others might have told you. **Your Father God needs you**. You are an important part of His plan for the world. You need a personal relationship with Him so you can know what His will is for your life. Jeremiah 29:11 states this very well.

"For I know the plans I have for you, declares the Lord, plans for welfare and not for evil, to give you a future and a hope."

There is a specific time and purpose for everything, as it says in Ecclesiastes 3:1 KJV.

"For everything there is a season, and a time to every purpose under heaven."

All persons have a particular assignment to do in their lifetimes. There are specific purposes for the specific times that each person lives in. This is by God's divine plan, not happenstance. You are alive right now because God has a special assignment just for you in this particular time in history.

If you are a true disciple of God and doing His will, you will not leave this earth until you have completed your assignment.

WHAT IS GOD'S WILL? – God's will is His divine plan. That's how He created things to be. Unfortunately, that divine plan has been altered on earth because of Satan's lies and Adam and Eve's sin. He said this to me one day,

My first will for anyone, is related to what my Son did. My will for my Son was to be the Messiah for the world, the Redeemer."

Jesus told the people,

 "For I came down from heaven, not to do my will, but the will of Him who sent me." (John 6:38)

In that same conversation with the people, He also told them God's will for them.

"For this is the will of my Father that sent me, that everyone who looks on the Son, and believes in him, should have everlasting life, and I will raise him up on the last day." (John 6:40)

God's will is for all people to believe in Jesus as Redeemer and as Lord. God told me that this will is a sovereign will, and it determines where each person spends eternity. He said,

If a person ignores this will of mine, they will be lost for eternity.

Remember that God sent Jesus to be our redeemer, but if we don't believe in him as our redeemer, then we will not be redeemed, we'll stay unholy, and be separated from God for ever.

When we have that intimate relationship, we can know God's will for the world, because He's told us in the Bible, and the Holy Spirit can reveal it to us. He said to me,

You represent me on this earth, so live like it! Do my will; my will is what's done in heaven and should be done on earth. Is there any sickness in heaven? No. Do people have to earn anything in heaven? No. Does Satan have any authority in heaven? No. Because I have authority in heaven, you have authority on earth, because we are one. You are my children, so act like it. Use your authority to make things right. Uphold my name.

God also has certain things planned for each of our lives and can speak directly to us to let us know what His will is for each day.

God sent Jesus to be our Lord. God's will is for us to live holy lives, by making Jesus the lord of our lives. That is how salvation comes to us. If we don't make Him lord of our lives, we will never have a personal relationship with Him, let alone do His will. Jesus warns us of being false believers in Matthew 7:21,

"Not everyone who says to me, 'Lord, Lord', will enter the kingdom of heaven, but the one who does the will of my Father who is in heaven."

God's will is that every person comes to know the Lord. Remember, we are His hands and feet. His will can only be done through us, His people. If we're not willing to be His hands and feet, then we really don't believe in Jesus, because if we did, we would be like Jesus and do what He did. He HAS to be Lord of our lives.

There are many people, who say Jesus is lord of their lives, and they may do wonderful things, but they don't live like He is lord of their lives. They still live carnally in unholiness. Jesus warns us to beware of such people. We will know them by their "fruit", which is mentioned in Matthew 7:17 NIV,

"Likewise every good tree bears good fruit, but a bad tree bears bad fruit."

People can put on a good show in public, but then in their private lives, live the opposite, where they bear bad fruit. Sadly, some think that because they did good deeds, they are saved and don't have to give up their unholy ways of living. However, Jesus says otherwise in Matthew 7:22-23,

"On that day many will say to me, 'Lord, Lord, did we not prophesy in Your name, and cast out demons in Your name, and do many mighty works in Your name?' And then I will declare to them, "I never knew you, depart from me, you workers of lawlessness."

He never knew them because they had no personal relationship with Him. They never accepted Him as Lord. He must truly be the lord of their lives, or there is no salvation for them. That is so tragic. It breaks God's heart. He told me so.

I love each and every one of them as much as I love my Son. The thought of not spending eternity with them breaks my heart. I grieve for each one.

Are you a true believer? Is Jesus Lord of your life? Is your life a reflection of His? Do you have confidence in where you'll be spending eternity?

God also has permissive will. I'll let Him explain that to you:

My permissive will can be disobeyed without loss of salvation. But, people may suffer the consequences.

For example: My will is that you don't be drunk. (Ephesians 5:18) **"And do not get drunk with wine . . ."** *But if you choose to drive drunk, cause a crash and kill someone, you won't lose your salvation, but you will have to suffer the consequences, along with the family of the person you killed.*

67

Any time you elect to do your will instead of mine you risk health, peace, joy and may even suffer physical death. Why? Because you live in a fallen world that is influenced by Satan who wants to cause you harm or death. Only I can see the big picture, the hazards ahead. I know what's best.

When you choose to go against my will you've switched over to your carnal mind and have temporally shut me off in your life; your protector, your wisdom, your problem solver.

Please stay turned on to my Spiritual power and do my will, for your sake and for the sake of others.

A good way of knowing the general will of God is to look at the fifty commands of Jesus. If you do these things, you will have an abundant and blessed life.

THE FIFTY COMMANDS OF JESUS – These commands of Jesus are also God's will for us. Make a conscious effort to follow these commands:

The Fifty Commands Of Jesus

1. *Don't call Jesus Lord when you don't obey Him.* Luke 6:46, Matthew 7:21.

2. *Build on the rock of obedience to Jesus otherwise you will fall.* Matthew 7:24-27, Luke 6:47-49.

3. *Worship God alone.* Matthew 4:10b, Luke 4:8.

4. *Follow Jesus.* Matthew 4:19, 11:28-30, Mark 1:17, John 1:43,12:26, 10:27, 21:22b.

5. *Be salt and light to this world.* Matthew 5:13-16 Mark 9:50, Luke 11:33, 14:34. John 3:21.

6. *Don't call your brother a fool. Matthew 5:22, 12:36.*

7. *Practice instant reconciliation. Matthew 5:24-25.*

8. *Do not look with lust at another, this is adultery in the heart. Matthew 5:27-28.*

9. *Do not divorce and marry another, this is adultery. Matthew 5:32, 19:9, Mark 10:11-12.*

10. *Don't swear an oath. Matthew 5:33-37.*

11. *Do more than expected, go the 2nd mile. Matt 5:38-41.*

12. *Give to those that ask. Matthew 5:42, Luke 6:30, 38.*

13. *Love, bless and pray for your enemies. Matthew 5:43-48, Luke 6:27-29.*

14. *Quietly do good for God's praise alone. Matthew 6:1-4.*

15. *When you pray, fast or give do it secretly. Matt 6:5-6.*

16. *Don't use vain repetitions when praying. Matt 6:7-8, Mark 12:40.*

17. *Pray to God the Father. Matthew 6:9, John 16:23-24.*

18. *Don't be anxious. Matthew 6:25-32, Luke 12:22-30, John 14:1, 16:33.*

19. *Store your riches in heaven not on earth. Matthew 6:19-33, Luke 12:21, 31-34, John 12:25.*

20. *Judge not that you may not be judged. Matthew 7:1-5, Luke 6:37, 41-42, John 7:24.*

21. *Keep asking, seeking and knocking.* Matthew 6:9-11, 7:7-11, Luke 11:9-13.

22. *Treat others as you like to be treated.* Matthew 7:12, Luke 6:31.

23. *Don't waste time on argumentative people.* Mathew 7:6.

24. *Forgive others.* Matthew 6:12, 14-15, 18:21,   Mark 11:25-26, Lk 11:9-13.

25. *Let the dead bury their dead.* Matthew 8:22, Luke 9:6a.

26. *Don't fear people-fear God.* Matthew 10:28, 16:23, Luke 12:4-5.

27. *Confess Christ before men.* Matthew 10:32-33,   Mark 5:19, 8:38, Luke 9:26, 12:8-9.

28. *Take up your cross.* Matthew 10:38-39, 16:24-26,   Mark 8:34-37, Luke 9:23-26, 14:26-33.

29. *Beware of hypocrisy and greed.* Matthew 15:6-9, 23:28, Luke 6:41-42, 12:1b, 20:46-47.

30. *Privately rebuke a brother and if he repents forgive him.* Matthew 18:15, Luke 17:3-4.

31. *Pay your taxes and give to God what is his.* Matthew 22:21, Mark 12:17, Luke 20:25, 21:4.

32. *Love God and others.* Matthew 22:37-40, Mark 12:30-31, Luke 10:27, John 15:12, 13:34-35.

33. *Keep alert and watch for the 2nd coming.* Matthew 24:44,46, 50-51, Mark 14:62, Luke 12:35-40, 21:27-28.

34. *Honor God with all that you have been given.* Matthew 25:14-31, Luke 18:18.

35. *Minister to others as you would to Jesus Himself.* Matthew 25:34-46.

36. *Preach the Gospel and teach obedience.* Matthew 28:20, Mark 16:15, Luke 9:60b, John 21:15b, 16b, 17b.

37. *Repent of your sins.* Mark 1:15, Luke 13:3,5, Luke 15:7,10, 18-24.

38. *Believe in Jesus.* Mark 16:16, Luke 9:35, John 12:36, 6:29, 20:29, 14:6.

39. *Have childlike faith.* Mark 10:15, Luke 18:17, Matthew 9:29.

40. *Don't sell things in God's house.* Mark 11:15-17, John 2:16.

41. *Rejoice when you are persecuted.* Luke 6:22-23.

42. *Don't be distracted from hearing God's Word.* Luke 10:38-42.

43. *Act with compassion and not prejudice towards others.* Luke 10:30-37.

44. *Invite the poor to eat with you.* Luke 14:13-14.

45. *Humble yourself & take the lowest position.* Luke 14:8-11, 18:13-14, Matthew 23:12, 19:30.

46. *You must be born again.* John 3:3, John 3:5-8.

47. *Live in Me and live in My love.* John 8:31-32, John 15:4, 9

48. *Don't covet your brother's blessing.* Luke 12:13-15, 15:29-30

49. *Be baptized.* Matthew 28:19, Mark 16:16

50. *Strive for perfection.* Matthew 5:48, John 15:14 Article Source[9]

THE TEN COMMANDMENTS – God's original ten commandments are still applicable for today. Just think how much better the world would be if everyone just followed these. (Exodus 20:3-17)

1. **You shall have no other gods before me**. Anything that you put before God is your true god. That could be anything: money, another person, yourself, your job, etc.

2. **You shall not make for yourself any [graven] carved idol.** Graven means sculpted or carved. The Israelites got in BIG trouble when they sculpted a golden calf and worshiped it. (Read the story in Exodus 32) Any image that you pray to, or worship, that is NOT God, is idolatry.

3. **You shall not take the name of the Lord in vain**. This means that you use God's name inappropriately: as a cuss word, mocking Him, or as an exclamation – i.e. "OMG". In other words, you are disrespecting Him.

4. **Remember the Sabbath day and keep it holy**. He wants you to set aside a day where you can relax, let go of the worries of the week, and enjoy His company, spend time with your family, etc. This is a holy time for you. It's a day of recuperation.

5. **Honor your father and mother**. God said that he will give you long life if you honor your parents. He didn't say to honor them if they were nice, good parents, He said to honor them, period. Treat them with respect, even if they don't deserve it; just like He treats us with respect when we don't deserve it.

6. **You shall not murder.** This is a command that is very misunderstood today. In the original Hebrew language, "murder" is the correct translation, not "kill". Murder literally means *"the intentional, premeditated killing of another person with <u>malice</u>.*

   Malice is a form of evil intent that separates "murder" from "killing". Even today, there are acceptable forms of killing that lacks this kind of evil intent.[10] Self-defense would be an example, as well as punishment, like a death penalty. Accidental death is also included in the list.

7. **You shall not commit adultery.** The definition of adultery is *"voluntary sexual intercourse between a married person and a person who is not their spouse".* This is also one of Jesus' commands. He even gave an extended definition of adultery.

   "But I say to you that everyone who looks at a woman with full intent to lust after her has already committed adultery with her in his heart." (Matthew 5:28)

   God takes, very seriously, what's in our hearts, because we are supposed to have Jesus' heart. When you have replaced Jesus in your heart with something else, you've committed spiritual adultery against Him. Remember: We are His betrothed.

8. **You shall not steal.** Stealing is taking something that does not belong to you; Period. That would be things like a car, money, a pen or paper from work, or taking something from someone and rationalizing that it's ok because you'll pay them back. There are many people serving prison time for embezzlement who have said that very same thing to themselves.

9. **You shall not bear false witness against your neighbor.** This means lying about someone to accuse them. (Neighbor means anyone around you. Read the parable of the Good Samaritan in Luke 10:25-37.)

10. **You shall not covet.** This is an obsessive desire to have what someone else has, oftentimes leading to theft or even adultery. This is another heart issue.

Can you imagine what the world would be like if we lived our lives according to God's will?

"This is the will of God, that by doing good you should put to silence the ignorance of foolish people." (I Peter 2:15)

Don't lose heart if you've broken any of these commands. God knows we are going to mess up; He just wants us to repent as soon as we realize we've messed up, so we can get back on track as soon as as possible.

First, and foremost: NEVER FORGET THAT GOD LOVES YOU!

Do you love Him? How do you know if you do? John 14:23 tells us what Jesus said about that?

"If you love me, you will keep my commandments."

 **"If you keep My commandments, you will abide in My love; just as I have kept my Father's commandments and abide in His love".** John 15:10

Lord, I know I mess up sometimes, and I thank You that You've forgiven me. I will try my best to follow your commandments so that I can be who I was created to be, and pass Your love onto others. Amen.

Reach Out To Others

Our purpose is to help God bring more people into His kingdom, so they can spend eternity with Him, as His Ekklesia. His "Church" is not a building, but people. His will is to spend eternity with everyone. He told me this,

It breaks my heart when people reject me. However, I will never reject them. Please come back to me!

God wants to save at least one billion people in the world-wide revival that's beginning to happen right now. He needs us to be who we were made to be and do what we were made to do. He said it's the Glory inside us that makes it possible.

It's through my Glory that a person can do my will. And my will for them is to use the talents, wisdom and my glory to accomplish the purposes that I created them to do. That is what makes life fulfilling for them, even if they don't understand it.

Many people need to hear the "good news". This world is a very dark place right now, and it's only the light of Jesus that can dissipate that dark. We need to take His light into the darkness.

I had a vision about this.

> I was in a hexagonal shaped dark room, I could barely see. I saw an open door that led into more darkness. There were dust balls everywhere. On the opposite wall from the open door was another shut door. It had a deadbolt on it. I slid back the deadbolt and opened the door and the room was filled with light. I noticed that the dust balls were actually little devils of darkness. I grabbed a broom that was there and swept the devils out the dark door, then slammed it shut and locked it.

75

I looked around and saw that the room was empty and light was coming in through the open door.

I said, "Holy Spirit come in and fill this room up with your presence." Suddenly, I felt the presence of Holy Spirit filling the room up to overflowing out the door. Holy Spirit said, "Open the portals." I looked around and then I noticed that on every wall of the room there were smaller doors flush with the walls. They had no knobs. I didn't know how to open them. I must have looked puzzled, because Holy Spirit said, "Tell them to open." So I did, and the portal doors swung open and the light shone out the portals into the darkness, which got lighter and lighter as the light went deeper and deeper into it.

Then a voice said, "Don't close the portals again. Let my light shine as a beacon to the unsaved, and let it fill the earth with light." Then I started to see the scene as if through a camera lens, pulling back until I could see the outside of the room. It kept pulling back until I realized that I was seeing a lighthouse with light beams pouring out into the darkness.

This is what Jesus interpreted:

The room is your heart. You had an open door to the darkness of the world. When you opened my door, by repenting and unlocking it, my Spirit was able to fill the room with my light. You then were able to see the dark things in your heart and sweep them out. More importantly, you shut the dark door and locked it.

When you asked Holy Spirit to fill the room with his presence, he could, and did. He couldn't take my light into the darkness

*until you verbally told the portals to open. My Spirit was able
then, to go into the world of darkness and your heart became
a lighthouse beacon for others to see the way back to me.*

I learned two valuable lessons from that vision.

1. **We have to examine ourselves on a daily basis**,
   because it's so easy to let things of the world into our hearts.
   We have to stop opening the "dark doors" and open the
   portals, just as Jesus told me in my vision.

2. **We must call forth God's will**; verbally declare it aloud.
   Even Jesus' birth happened because people had voiced that
   for centuries.

So, to whom are we going to declare it?

FAMILY – It can be difficult to reach family members with God's
message. They don't see us as likely candidates for discipleship
because they just see us as who we've always been; Sis, Junior, Mom,
Dad, etc. Jesus even commented on this in Mark 6:4,

**"A prophet is not without honor, except in his own
hometown and among his relatives in his own household."**

The best way to minister to your family is to let them see Jesus in
you. Let them see how you've changed. Let them see God's peace,
joy and love through you. Bless them and tell them you love them
and God does, too. In other words, be the example.

PEOPLE WE ASSOCIATE WITH – The best way to get God's
message across to the people we work with, go to church with, play
sports with, a club we belong to, and such, is to be the example of
Jesus. Let them see a difference in your life from theirs. Make a
point to say hi to them, maybe compliment them in some way, tell
them it's good to see them, or how much you appreciate them.

You don't, or shouldn't, preach to them. You can answer a question they may have, or invite them to church or a picnic. Eventually, someone will be curious enough to ask you about why you're different. Then you can tell them about Jesus. Listen to the Holy Spirit's promptings.

PEOPLE WE DON'T KNOW – The people we don't know have never seen us, so they can't compare our lives now with the way it used to be. Therefore, the approach has to be different.

Even though you only have a few minutes, it's still important to break the ice, so to speak. Comment on something that you see: "I like your shirt. I love the colors." People usually respond. Pay attention to what they say, and then comment on that. If you can find common ground somewhere, that's even better.

If they have a need that you're aware of, help them if you can. If they say that you don't have to, say something like, "I know, I just want to because God has really blessed me this month, so I'm just sharing some of it." Now the door is open. Throw a little prayer to Holy Spirit to show you if there's anything else you can say or do. When you leave, tell them, "God bless you."

THE HOMELESS – Don't ignore the homeless. Give them some change if you have some, or buy them a meal, or give them a bottle of water or something. You might say to them that you've had some hard times yourself (which most people have.) Tell them that people helped you, so You're paying it forward by helping others. Listen to Holy Spirit's direction.

 Maybe you have time to sit and talk with them for a while. Some of them would enjoy it. It's probably been a while since anyone has treated them with respect. Again, ask for the Holy Spirit's help.

I once pulled up to a stoplight and a woman had a sign that said, "fallen on hard times, need food for my kids." I didn't have any money to give to her but, I did give her a bottle of water and a bag of apples I had just bought. She seemed so appreciative for it. I was glad I could help.

In these scenarios, you are planting seeds; Holy Spirit will water them. Your goal isn't to "save" people, that's the Holy Spirit's job. Your job is to be a reflection of Jesus, a "little Christ" to them. In all of these cases, find a personal need they have and meet it if you can. This is critical to their salvation. They must see God's love at work.

PEOPLE WITH SPECIFIC NEEDS – When you are going to help people with a particular issue, like a back problem, it's still nice to break the ice. Give them your first name, and ask what theirs is. You may even tell them why you're there.

Ask them about their issue; how long it's been an issue and how bad the pain is from 1 to 10. Ask the Holy Spirit if He has anything to tell you about that person. Tell them, "God loves you and He wants to show you how much He loves you. He wants you whole." Then use your authority to heal the person. Listen to the Holy Spirit's promptings. Each situation is different.

This book isn't designed to be a manual on how to minister, it's meant to help God's people, the body of Christ, to become the Light that it was ordained, and supposed to be. I recommend that you read books and watch videos that are available from people who have been ministering for some time. See the Study Materials section in the back of this book.

Matthew 5:16

"In the same way, let your light shine before others, so that they may see your good works and give glory to our Father. . ."

Help me Holy Spirit to let my light shine, so that I can bring the light of Jesus into this dark world. Amen.

Why We Need to Reach Out

God says we need to reach out. There are several reasons why.

BECAUSE HE SAID SO – in Philippians 2:4. **"Let each of you look not only at your own interests, but also to the interests of others."** Jesus says, **"Go into all the world and proclaim the gospel to the whole creation."** He says that in Mark 16:15.

When we give our lives to God, it doesn't end there. We must do God's will as well. He wants every person to have the same chance that we had, and His people are the ones that have to tell them. God told me this in one of our conversations.

I am counting on my people to see others as I do, for having my heart's desire for them and for being "little Christs" to the world. Time is so short and the harvest so great. I need every person of mine to activate his or her spirits and run the race and fight the battle. Show the people of the world my heart, how much I love them and value them, how much I want to be with them and take care of them. They are beautiful and precious to me.

Remember that when we aren't doing God's will, we may suffer consequences. One of the reasons that God had me write this book is because He is not pleased with His Church, and He's letting us know why. This is what He told me,

I can only exercise my authority through humans, because they have the earth suits to interact within the earthly realm. I have authority on earth; it's part of my creation, but it manifests in the earthly realm when a human calls it forth; declares it, then acts on it. They do that by faith.

Most of the world thinks I have no authority on earth because most of my people have not called it forth. As a result, Satan has run amuck. The people of the world think they have their own authority to solve their own problems, but it's really Satan that's calling the shots. He wants them to believe that they have their own authority, and may "solve" the problem without telling them. However, it comes at a very serious cost; fear, confusion, deception, chaos, anarchy, domination and eventual death, which is separation from me.

People believe they only answer to themselves, so they don't think they have to answer to anyone else. They have confidence that they can do whatever they want without suffering consequences. Of course, they will have to answer to ME at some point.

Satan has blinded them and they don't realize that He's in control. They will follow anyone that appears to believe the way they do. What they don't understand is that they are being deceived and manipulated by people who know perfectly well that Satan is calling the shots, because they have actually given their authority over to him; they've made a pact with him. They have chosen to give their lives to him.

God grieves for the people that have given their lives over to Satan. He misses them because He still loves them and always will. But, at some point a judgment will come upon them.

Church, do you really understand that they will all answer to me in the end? I'm the one with the REAL authority. They will spend eternity in hell, with NO HOPE! Church, do you really think this is what I want? Church, I love each of them as much as I love my Son! I want to spend eternity with them and take care of them. However, they don't know that because none of my people have told them. Or, they don't believe it because they don't think I have any authority to make it happen.

Why is that Church? You have not exercised your authority on my behalf. Them? They will have to "live" with the consequences of their decisions, which were based on Satan's lies, not my Truth. My people are accountable, because they did not show them my Truth. Notice I didn't say "tell" them the Truth. I said "show" them the Truth. There's quite a difference. Showing the Truth is living it!

So do it Church! Show them that I have authority over every lousy, dark thing in their lives. Make my will be done on earth as it is in heaven.

Oh my . . . we have fallen very short of our responsibilities as children and disciples of God. We'd better get our acts together or we're going to be in BIG trouble.

PEOPLE ARE SO HUNGRY FOR THE TRUTH – The people of this world search their whole lives to find something to fill the void inside of them. It's a void that only God can fill, and it's only through God's Truth that they will find it. God told me the following:

The world is so hungry for my Truth. People need to understand that they don't have to live under the binding constraints of the world. They can have an abundant life; a supernatural life if they would just realize what Jesus accomplished on the cross and by his resurrection. They must understand that wholeness is only possible with me living within them. My people must show them.

(Note: God told me that His own people must understand what he said in the last paragraph; most of them do not.)

How are we, the Church supposed to show others the benefits of being a child of God if we don't understand it ourselves! We need to wake up.

JESUS SUFFERED AND DIED FOR THEM – I think we have a tendency to forget the tremendous sacrifice Jesus made on our behalf, on ALL people's behalf. If it wasn't for that, this book would not have been written, and we would all be spending eternity in hell instead of with our heavenly Father.

I had an interesting conversation with God about what Jesus really accomplished with his sacrifice. I must say that God is so proud of His Son and is very grateful for what His Son did. He told me,

I had to send my Son to exchange his righteousness for the sins of the world. He had to be human for that to happen. The problem was, if he was born from a human couple, he would have been born in sin and that would have defeated the purpose. So he had to be born of a woman, to be human, but conceived by my Holy Spirit who has no sin. By that, Yeshua was able to interact in the world, as a human, but he was sinless because he wasn't a seed of Adam.

Now, Yeshua could have chosen the sinful, worldly way to live, but gratefully, he chose to live a righteous life, which made him a perfect sacrificial lamb to atone for humankind's sins. By his suffering and death, Yeshua traded his righteousness for humans' sins. These sins were buried when he was laid in the tomb.

When I raised Yeshua from the dead, he overcame death. He is now alive and anyone who believes that he is my Son and Messiah, they, too, can have eternal life with me, for now my Spirit lives in them, because they are now holy. My Son and they are now one, so they are one with me, because they chose him."

As God was talking, I could hear the pride in his voice. He is such a doting father. The amazing thing is that I have heard that in His voice when we have conversations about me. Wow . . . He continues,

> *Yeshua became the door to my kingdom, and opened the way for anyone who chooses to live their lives as a child of mine. When they do, they are no longer bound by the restraints of the physical world, because the Holy Spirit lives in them and now takes care of them, just as he took care of Adam and Eve in the Garden of Eden.*

> *Sadly, most of my people don't understand this. Thankfully, there is a remnant that is searching out the Truth and starting to live it. I thank them for that and am grateful. I bless them greatly.*

GOD HAS A MESSAGE THAT NEEDS DELIVERED - One day I thanked God for helping me make a coffee bar out of an old cupboard that I had fixed up. It was ratty, but fixed up pretty well. Then I decided to make it into a coffee bar, and now it looks like a completely new cupboard. It just goes to show that something that people don't have a use for and throw away, can be rescued and repaired and even made into something new.

I compared that to what the Lord does with people that society has discarded. He takes persons that are unwanted and thrown out, that's broken and dirty and rescues them from the trash heap of this world. He cleans them up, repairs their broken hearts and makes them into new people, who are whole, beautiful, and so wanted by Him, so loved by Him. This is how He responded,

I created every single person ever conceived out of my love. They were created for a special purpose, and just because they are broken and dirty, doesn't mean they are forgotten by me. Remind people that I'M not the one that's thrown them out; the world has done that. I want to rescue

them and make them new again, for their purpose is still here and my love is still upon them.

Tell them that Jesus took their ugliness upon himself so that they can become new beautiful people, loved by us and cherished so much. Tell them they don't have to stay broken. Shalom.

We have to remember that He did that for us. He took us broken people, made us new again, and accepted us into His family.

This is the message that God wants us to carry into the world. Everyone is important to Him. He said to me,

Church, show others my love for them. Let them know how I've blessed you, and then tell them how I want to bless them.

Luke 6:9

"Father, hallowed be your name. Your kingdom come, Your will be done, on earth, as it is in heaven."

Thank You for making me a brand new person, and for loving me. Help me to trust in who I am as Your child. I will do all I can to bring Your love to the lost souls so that they may know You, too. I love You. Amen.

CHAPTER 4

THE RESTORATION OF GOD'S CHURCH

Within this book, God has already expressed His dissatisfaction with us, His Church. We have let Him down. However, we have let the people of the world down as well. How many of them are suffering in hell, separated from their Creator for all eternity, because we haven't done what we were created to do, or been who we were created to be, little Christs? God told me this,

The difference between Jesus and his disciples was that Jesus had the Holy Spirit indwelling him; Jesus had no unholiness in his heart and Holy Spirit could exist there.

The disciples were from the seed of Adam and were unholy, not holy like Jesus, and were under the curse of death. Jesus had to take his light, my presence to the disciples so they could do what Jesus did. They lived FOR my presence; Jesus lived FROM my presence because he already had me in him as the Holy Spirit.

When Jesus accomplished his mission, he redeemed people by exchanging his righteousness (me) for their sins. That meant that my Spirit could live in them since they were now holy. The disciples could now do what Jesus

had done, without Him being there, because my presence was in them. From then on they lived FROM my presence just as Jesus had done.

Why the Church Has Become So Broken

Something that needs restoration has to be broken. When something is broken, it can't function the way it was designed to. That's happened to the Church. How has the Church become so broken? God continued His message to me,

Anyone who accepts Jesus as the Messiah, now has my Spirit living in them which means that they should be living FROM my presence just as the disciples did in my young Church. Unfortunately, most of my people are still trying to live FOR my presence. They don't know the Truth because my message has been watered down and filled with half-truths and lies.

SATAN HAS INFILTRATED THE CHURCH - Satan has tried to destroy the Church from the beginning. He tried to destroy Jesus' mission before He was even born. Satan knew that the Messiah would come from the Hebrew nation, so he knew if he could keep the Hebrews in bondage, they wouldn't go to the land God had promised them. So, Satan manipulated the Pharaoh to murder all of the Hebrew newborn baby boys. Thankfully, Pharaoh's own daughter thwarted his plan. (Read the story in Exodus 1:15-22).

Fourteen-hundred forty-three years later, Satan tried to do the same to Jesus. He used Herod as a tool to destroy Jesus by murdering all the baby boys from 2 years old and under in the town where Jesus and His parents lived. This time an angel thwarted Satan by telling Jesus' parents to flee. (Read about it in Matthew 2:13-18)

Thirty-one years later, Satan finally thought he'd won. This is what God said to me,

From the beginning Satan tried to wipe my Church out. He thought he did when Jesus was killed on a cross. (Chuckling) He didn't realize the he was actually instrumental in my ability to carry out my plan of salvation. I find that humorous. Satan didn't. He stepped up his attacks on my Church. There was great persecution, and many members of my young Church were murdered.

In Acts 7-8 is the story of Stephen who was stoned to death for his faith, by the Hebrew religious leaders. He's considered by many to be the first Christian martyr. A young Pharisee there consented to Stephen's death, and was instrumental in a great persecution against the Church. God continued His message to me,

(Chuckling again) I also find it humorous that one of Satan's most ardent supporters of his persecution of the Church became one of MY most important advocates; Saul, which I renamed Paul. (Read about it in Acts 9)

Satan finally realized that he wasn't able to destroy my Church, so he switched to a new tactic: infiltration. He knew if he could infiltrate the Church with his people, he could water down my message with half-truths that contained just enough truth that the people would believe it. Of course, My people didn't take the time to study the scriptures to find out if his words were 'truth, and nothing but the truth.

The book of Jude in the Bible deals with the false teachings of the infiltrators. Jude appeals to **"those who are sanctified and called by God the Father and preserved in Jesus the Messiah."** That is Jude 1:1.

He found it necessary to write to them and plead for them to fight for the faith which was originally given to Jesus disciples, because the message had been so changed by Satan's infiltrators. He says, in Jude 1:4,

"For certain people have crept in unnoticed who were long ago designated for this condemnation, ungodly people, who pervert the Grace of our God into sensuality and deny the only Master and Lord, Jesus Christ."

It didn't take long for Satan to accomplish his goal: Jude was written between 70 AD to 90 AD. Jude called these false teachers, in Jude 1:12, **clouds without water, carried along by winds; autumn trees without fruit, twice dead, uprooted; raging waves of the sea, which are foaming up their own shame; wandering stars for whom the gloom of darkness has been kept forever.**

God said to me,

As a result, the word being taught in the churches has become so watered down and filled with untruths that my Church has become mostly ineffective and nearly powerless.

No wonder the world is so dark, chaotic, dangerous and LOST!

THE CHURCH HAS BECOME TOO WORLDLY - When we become a child of God, we are supposed to live like a child of God. If you don't know what that is, then look at Jesus, God's only begotten son. Our lives are to be a reflection of His. In other words, we should live in holiness. In one of our conversations, God said this to me,

People need to know that you are my children and are blessed. And they know that because your lives are different from theirs. They are watching everything. Are your lives different from theirs? Or are you sick, confused, and discouraged just like them. You can't make a difference in someone else's life until THEY SEE SOMETHING DIFFERENT IN YOURS.

If there is no difference between the people of the world and us, then we are too worldly. We're living from our carnal minds and letting the physical realm dominate us instead of putting our trust in the Lord and living from His Spirit.

I have a question for you, one I asked myself. Did you ever think to yourself that there *must* be something more? If you've ever thought that, then you are living too much in the world. It's taken me a decade to finally understand that. That's how long I've been searching for an answer to that question, "Is there something more?

The sad part is we don't know that we are living too worldly. I had to learn that from God Himself, because I grew up in religion, the watered down version of God's Word. We've been lied to by Satan.

I know that there are sincere leaders of the Church, people who take their calling seriously, and God appreciates that and so do I. However, they grew up and studied with a watered down word.

(Note: I originally wrote Word, with a capital W, but God told me to change it to lowercase, because, what is being taught in our churches is more of the world's word than His Word.)

Ouch . . . God has forgiven us but we must repent. If you are one of the leaders of the Church, you need to go back to the **W**ord and open your spiritual mind so the Holy Spirit can teach you the **T**ruth. It will set you free from the constraints of this world and let you soar!

Jude had warnings in his writings, so does God. This is a warning He gave to me referencing Revelation 3:16.

Yeshua is going to spit out the people of the Church that are not doing my will. And he's starting with the leaders; especially the under shepherds: ministers, preachers, pastors, etc. He needs to get them out of the way, so that people can hear the Truth, the WHOLE Truth. It's starting now!

Examine yourself, so you won't be judged. Repent, before it's too late!

THE CHURCH IS COLLUDING WITH THE ENEMY – If this heading wasn't in uppercase, I would use the non-capitalized version of "church", because God says that the religionized church is not of Him. Many leaders of the religions are actually colluding with Satan. They are intentionally opposing God and His divine plan, all for a reward of power and wealth.

God said this to me,

These leaders are also intentionally leading my people astray. Most of them say one thing to their members and do the opposite themselves. Unfortunately, my people don't realize it because they are still thinking with their carnal minds instead of reasoning with their spirits, powered by the Holy Spirit.

In Matthew 7:15, God warned us to be aware of these people. **"Beware of false prophets, which come to you in sheep's clothing, but inwardly are ravenous wolves."**

These unholy leaders aren't just helping Satan push his agenda, they are also committing some of the most despicable and evil acts known to mankind, especially to my little ones!

Have I not said that it would be better for a person to have a millstone hung on his neck and be thrown into the depth of the sea than to offend one of my little ones! (Read that in Matthew 18:6.)

YOU WILL ANSWER TO ME!!

The world's children are being sacrificed to the most shameful, despicable acts: including kidnapping, rape, human trafficking, sexual perversion, mental and physical torture and even death.

Romans 1:32 says these people know the truth, but choose not to live it. **"Though they know God's decree that those that practice such things deserve to die, they not only do them but give approval to those that practice them."**

That verse applies to many church leaders. Do they assume that because they are "church leaders" they are off the hook? Well, God answered that question three paragraphs ago.

THE CHURCH IS ENABLING THE ENEMY - Because of the deceit and the watering down of God's message, most of His people, as mentioned earlier, are ineffective and nearly powerless, to the point that they can't do anything.

Well, when we do nothing to stop Satan's agenda, when we don't take a stand against him, we are actually enabling him. God mentioned this in one of our conversations:

My people enable Satan, by not doing anything. Because no one is pushing him back, Satan's agenda is accomplished; he has no resistance. He is able to march through the ranks unchallenged. That's the main reason the world is in such dire, terrifying conditions.

If my Church doesn't get off its collective butts (His word not mine, I asked)*, leave the four walls of the church buildings and show the world my love – being "little Christs" to them – well . . . if you think it's bad now . . .*

That's where He left it hang. I think we're intelligent enough to fill in the rest of the sentence. It's imperative that we, God's Church, start being who we were created to be and do what we were created to do. Why don't we?

We're afraid – Remember, God's perfect Love casts out fear.

We feel powerless – We have everything that we need: God's power, His love, His authority right inside of us.

We don't know what to do – God's Holy Word is available 24/7, along with His Holy Spirit to teach us, and the life of Jesus is an example of how to live.

We don't know God's will – That's why He wants a personal relationship with us, so we can find out what His will is. He has important things for us to do.

We think we're too old. Here's what God had to say about that in a short conversation we had. I had a thought pop in my mind that I'm old to be learning these things.

> *You just thought to yourself that you're too old to learn all this. It was a flash thought, from Satan. Remember that 68 years is barely a "flash" in eternity. You now live in eternity with me (no beginning and no ending), so trust me when I say that you're not old. As a matter of fact, you'll never be old again.*

> Is that why everyone in heaven looks like they're in their late 20's or early 30's?

> *Yes; Prime of life. My people on earth may look like they're "old" because they don't have their glorified bodies yet, but they don't act like it if they are doing my will, the purpose I have ordained for them. They're vibrant and love what they are doing.*

> That's true. I can hardly wait to get up in the morning and get back to typing Your words. I don't feel old, just . . . vibrant like you said.

Remember, God told us earlier, we need to look at things from His point-of-view, from eternity. That gives us a whole new perspective on things like age. I had never thought about that before.

This is what God says,

It's time for my Church to start living from my presence, instead of for my presence. My presence, my Glory, is already inside of you. It's time to stop making excuses, and go take that power, change your lives and do my will. I am counting on you all to free lost people for my kingdom. I love you and love others through you."

"WAKE UP CHURCH! TIME IS VERY SHORT!"

Proverbs 14:12

"There is a way that seems right to a man, but its end is a way to death."

Help me Lord to keep my eye on You and not the things of this world. Help me to search the Word, Holy Spirit, so that I can discern false teachings, and not follow Satan's corrupt ways. Help me to know Your will, so I can stand against the evil in the world. Help me, Holy Spirit, to learn the Truth so I can tell others and they can be set free. In Jesus name, I pray. Amen.

How to Restore the Church

The only hope for the people of this world is the Church; a Church that is vibrant, bold, fearless and has the heart of Jesus. I asked God how we go about restoring the Church to His original design. He gave me some steps that we, His Church need to do.

UNDERSTAND HOW THE CHURCH WAS ORIGINALLY SET UP – The "Church" today is very different from what Jesus originally set up. That's because of Satan's infiltration. He cannot afford to let us understand our heritage as the "Church" as it was intended, because, it was very effective. It wasn't a religious institution, it was an ekklesia, a secular institution.

The Ekklesia didn't meet in buildings, but in the marketplace of everyday life. It was open primarily to every Jewish person, including women. Because the members "preached" outdoors, anyone could hear their message, which dealt with the issues in people's lives. As a result, the members, starting with Jesus and just twelve men in Jerusalem, increased to thousands.

After Pentecost, the Ekklesia started ministering to Gentiles as well as the Jews, and as a result, within a three-year period, every person in the entire region of the Roman Empire in Asia, had heard the "Good News", as it says in Acts 19:10.

". . . all the residents of Asia heard the Word of the Lord, both Jews and Greeks."

Why were they able to spread the Word to over a million people in a thirty thousand square mile area, in three years with no cars, trains, planes, phones or the internet? It was because they were a part of an organization open to all people. Each member ministered to the populace in their sphere of influence. As each person joined the Ekklesia, they became ministers as well.

They ministered 24/7 by living their lives as a reflection of Jesus. It wasn't religion, it was a lifestyle. In other words, they were full-time ministers of God's Kingdom.

When Jesus told Peter that he was the rock (foundation), He didn't say "of the church", He said "of His Ekklesia". What's the difference?

Ekklesia means assembly: *ek (out of), klesis 'a calling' (kaleo, 'to call'); a calling out of citizens from their homes to a public place.* The practice of *ekklesia* had been in use for approximately 500 years by the time of Christ. It was a principle assembly of citizens of a kingdom, and they were part of the ruling counsel of that government.

The ekklesia was responsible for military and governmental matters, including electing generals and government officials, declaring war and overseeing military strategies. They voted on decrees, treaties and law proposals. They met 3 or 4 times a month.

The ekklesia members were so important to the governing of the nation, that if two or three were gathered together somewhere in another jurisdiction, they were considered a Conventus, and could conduct governmental business on behalf of the Emperor. It was considered that He was actually present at that place through the Conventus.

Jesus was going to set up His own governmental assembly. He told Peter that in Matthew 16:18,

"And I tell you, you are Peter and on this rock I will build my Ekklesia." (Strongs: G1577 (εκκληαια) **ekklésea.)**

Through His Ekklesia, He addressed spiritual and physical issues by meeting the physical needs of the population. This allowed people to see that God truly loved them, cared about them and wanted them to be a part of His family.

The Ekklesia represents God's Kingdom on earth. We are a part of God's ruling counsel. That is why Jesus told them that wherever two or three Ekklesia members met they could conduct business on behalf of God's Kingdom. They were His Conventus, and as such, He was considered there among them.

The term "church" was never In the original language. Ekklesia or assembly is used 115 times in the New Testament, but translated as "church" in all but three of those times. (Acts 19:32, 39, 41.)

The word "church" comes from Old English cir(i)ce, related to Dutch kerk, and German Kirche, based on medival Greek kuriakon.

"Church" relates to a building where certain people go at certain times to be ministered to by a particular priest or pastor. The messages and activities are primarily centered around the members.

It is important that members meet together for studying, teaching and encouragement, and to plan strategy and pray together to address specific issues. However, they MUST leave the church building and be ministers in the marketplace; a lifestyle of ministering, and representing God's kingdom on earth as part of His ruling counsel. This is how Jesus set up His Ekklesia.

That hasn't happened in most modern churches. Because of Satan's infiltration, God's people do not know the real purpose of the "Church" (the Body of Christ). They've been misled by manmade doctrines of the church hierarchy, going back centuries. Just like the priests in Jesus' time, they wanted power, and didn't want any challenges to their "right" to rule through the church.

This ideal was "cemented" in place by none other than King James of the King James Bible fame. He believed in the right of Kings to have total reign, secular and religious, and they were able to do that by reigning through priests of the church, which were appointed and supported by the king.

King James did not like the fact that the common people were able to make decisions, minister and help meet the needs of others, through an ekklesia type assembly. He wanted everyone to be dependent upon the government, him, for everything in their lives.

(Sound familiar?)

At the time, some English versions of the Bible translated "ekklesia" as "assembly", which it was. People in power did not like that, and King James decided to have a translation of the Bible, based on the original text, which is good, except, he told his scribes to translate "assembly" as "church".

Then he decreed that his Bible was the official translation. And for most modern churches it is. Most modern translations of the Bible also use the word "church" instead of assembly or ekklesia.

It is very CRITICAL that God's people learn about the Ekklesia and understand how it functions and how it affects people's lives. It is what separates us from the rest of the world. (See STUDY MATERIALS for a list of available materials on this topic.)

God talked to me, in a conversation we had, about how the Church is split.

When Yeshua created the Ekklesia, He kept the Scriptural teachings and principles of the Temple, and the gathering and fellowship of the Tabernacle. He blended them in His secular Ekklesia.

What has religion done to the Body of Christ? It has separated us into different churches with different philosophies and traditions. Some of the churches address the importance of gathering and fellowshipping, the social issues of life. These are known as the liberal churches. Some address the importance of spiritual issues and of Scripture. These are known as the conservative churches. And there is a great wall between them. It's almost like they are at war with each other.

Unless the Churches unite in a common cause and start to work together, there will only be half-work being done, and systematic poverty cannot be eradicated. It is the outcome of Adam's sin.

There are four dimensions of systematic poverty that must be addressed: motivational, relational, material and spiritual. The Ekklesia addressed all four. When they gathered and blessed people, they addressed the motivational dimension. When they fellowshipped with people, they addressed the relational dimension. These are the social issues.

When they ministered to people (met their needs) they addressed the material dimension. When they proclaimed my Kingdom was at hand, they addressed the spiritual dimension. These are the fundamental issues.

All four must be dealt with to abolish poverty. This is why governmental programs will not eradicate poverty. They only address the material dimension. Religion will not eradicate poverty. It only addresses the material and spiritual dimensions in the conservative churches, or the material and relational dimensions in the liberal churches.

My Ekklesia addresses all four of these dimensions. Find an Ekklesia and be an active member, ask the Holy Spirit's help in finding an ekklesia, or start one right where you are. When you become a part of My Ekklesia, You will finally know the "more" and what your purpose is. You will finally be who you were created to be and do what you were created to do."

Thank You Lord for teaching us the Truth!

(Note: If you want a sense of what the Ekklesia did, watch the series *The Chosen.* You can access it through the app.[11] This has helped me to understand what Jesus and His Ekklesia was all about.)

TRULY UNDERSTAND WHAT JESUS DID FOR US – I really believe that most of us truly don't understand this. I didn't until God and I had conversations about it. He wants me to share one of them with you.

> If Jesus hadn't been willing to give up his righteousness for my sin, then I would be spending eternity in hell?
>
> *Yes. My Son didn't want to suffer like he had to. He agonized about it so much that he sweated blood as he prayed to me the night before his arrest. He even asked me if there was another way. There wasn't. He was the only one worthy. Read the verses from Revelation 5:1-3 that speaks of that.*

"Then I saw in the right hand of him who was seated on the throne, a scroll written within and on the sides and sealed with seven seals. And I saw a mighty angel proclaiming with a loud voice, "Who is worthy to open the scroll and break its seals?"

"And no one in heaven or earth or under the earth was able to open the scroll or look into it." NIV

My Son volunteered, and the assembly vetted him and found him worthy. Read verses 6-7.

"Then I saw a lamb, looking as if it had been slain, standing in the center of the throne, encircled by the four living creatures and the elders. He had seven horns and seven eyes, which are the seven spirits of God sent out into all the earth. He went and took the scroll from the right hand of Him who sat on the throne." NIV

Yeshua volunteered to give up his divinity to become a man.

"He made himself nothing by taking the very nature of a servant, being made in human likeness." This is from Philippians 2:7, the NIV translation. Another translation said he emptied himself.

Yes, he was worthy, but at any time he could have refused to do what needed to be done. It wasn't just the torture he agonized over, it was the fact that he knew that if he gave up his righteousness (me, his Father) we would be separated. That really bothered him because there was never a time

when we weren't together. I am so grateful that he did my will and not his own.

Me too, Lord!

(Note: In Chapter 1 is the explanation of how righteousness is actually the presence of God. Reread that if you are still confused about this.)

Do you know when the exchange between your sin and his righteousness occurred?

When he cried, "Why have you forsaken me?"

Yes, that is when you became worthy to be with me, because at that point Yeshua took your sin upon himself.

But, if we have no sin, then why don't we all just automatically spend eternity with You?

I gave my creation free will. Not everyone chooses to accept that marvelous sacrifice that Yeshua made. They have a right to reject Yeshua's righteousness. And when they do, they are essentially rejecting me. Those that reject me will spend eternity without me, in the only place where my blessings are not: hell; a place where Satan will spend eternity because he rejected me . . .

There was a brief silence, then, with great sadness, He spoke again,

He was the first of many . . .

That makes you so sad.

Yes, I love all of my creation, especially humans, for you were created to be with me. And, I so miss the people that have rejected me. I will never reject them, but there will come a time in their lives when they will be separated from me for all eternity. . . (sighs). I cannot exist where unholiness is.

Oh, boy . . . and they spend eternity in agony because there is no goodness there . . .

That's right, because goodness comes from me.

He sighed again.

There is no hope there.

I tell you all this, because my people need to understand why Jesus did what He did, and why they are now worthy to have a personal relationship with me; we are one! However, it must be a spiritual relationship because I am not human, I am spirit. I have no earth suit.

Please wake up, Church. Be my Ekklesia. Seek a personal relationship with me. I need you. The world needs your light. You are worthy to pass on my message to others. You are worthy because of Yeshua's sacrifice. Don't EVER forget that!

We owe our lives to Jesus.

UNDERSTAND THE DIFFERENCE BETWEEN WORLDLY AND SPIRITUAL – One thing we have to understand is the difference between two realms, the worldly realm and the spiritual realm. Your essence, your being exists in the spiritual realm; your body exists in the natural or worldly realm. God told me,

Your spirit comes from my eternal realm. Unfortunately, because of Adam and Eve's sin, the spirits of humans went dormant because I withdrew my Holy Spirit from them. I cannot exist with sin. Their carnal minds took over, since my Spirit was not there to sustain them anymore.

My Son came to earth as a human so he could become the atonement for humankind's sins. When he did that he made it possible for humans to connect back up with my Holy Spirit, awaken their spirits and experience eternity again. It's my presence that brings eternity into the worldly realm.

This is such a hard concept for people to understand, more so for Christians than others, I think. I believe it's part of the deception of Satan that has caused this. He will do anything he can to keep us from understanding who we are in Christ. If we realize who we really are, and the authority we have in the spiritual realm, he knows that he will be undone.

I still needed some clarity. God did some more explaining.

I created the physical realm from my imagination. I wanted humans to enjoy my creation. A spirit doesn't have physical arms and legs, so I had to give people a body so that their spirits could interact in the natural realm. I call it an earth suit.

Your spirit is who you are, your essence. You were spirit before you were human. You became human when I created your body and breathed your spirit inside it. Adam and Eve knew they were spirit first. They lived from their spirits, interconnected to me through my Holy Spirit. They had their switches turned on. It was through their spirits that we could spend time together, talk and enjoy each other's company.

Adam and Eve used their bodies, their earth suits, to interact with the animals and plants, etc. I so enjoyed their company, but I also took great pleasure in watching them interact with the natural realm, just as any good father does when he sees his children enjoying a gift that he had given them.

There is one more thing you must realize: God is NOT in control of the worldly realm, Satan is. I know, I know that's not what you've been taught, but nevertheless it's true. Even God's disciples admitted that in I John 5:19,

"We know that we are from God, and the whole world lies in the power of the evil one."

God can't control what Satan does in the world, because God can't interact in the worldly realm, like Jesus and us. So, God's will and authority can only manifest on the earth through His people. He has to rely on us. The question is, *can* He rely on us?

I gave humans authority over the earthly realm. When Adam and Eve sinned, they handed over their authority to Satan by doing his will instead of mine.

Even though Jesus redeemed our authority, we've not been using it because we figured that God had it covered, He was in control. That's what we've been told; another lie from Satan.

The world is in terrible shape. Do you actually think that's what God wants? No, He doesn't want the world to be in terrible shape, it's in this condition because WE, His people, have not taken authority over the gates of hell, Satan's domain. We are still thinking like church people instead of living like His Ekklesia.

Because most humans are natural beings, they know nothing of the spiritual realm, unless they believe in the occult or spiritualism. Since humankind essentially handed their authority over to Satan, he controls what goes on in the worldly realm, by planting thoughts into people's minds. Because they have no discernment from Holy

Spirit, they latch onto those thoughts, dwelling on them until they become reality to them.

Our bodies are dependent on our spirits. They wouldn't exist otherwise. Our spirits have authority over our bodies if we stay turned on to Holy Spirit's power. Let me give you an example of what happens when we don't take thoughts captive.

Because of the beating that Jesus suffered on our behalf, we were healed, as stated in Isaiah 53:5,

"But He was wounded for our transgressions, He was bruised for our iniquities; the chastisement of our peace was upon Him, and by His stripes we are healed." KJV

Our healings are already a done deal in the spiritual realm. But when it comes to healing we think our bodies have authority over our spirits. So, instead of speaking life, affirming our healing, we focus on the symptoms we're feeling, which start as thoughts in our minds:

> "Hmm . . . I think I have kind of a headache." Well, then you think, "If I have a headache I may have a fever." Then you feel your brow and it feels hot. You take your temperature and sure enough, you have a fever, and to top it off your headache is worse. Then you think, "If I have a fever then I must have an infection somewhere."
>
> Then you focus on where an infection could be. "Hmm . . . my throat has been kind of scratchy today and I sound a little hoarse." You swallow and then think, "There seems to be a little pain in the back of my throat." So you take a pain pill. You swallow again and think, "Ooo, my throat is really sore. I can barely swallow. I better check it out."

You look in the mirror and notice that your throat is red and think, "Are those white spots that I see? Oh, man, don't tell me I'm getting strep throat! Well, a pain pill won't help that."

So, you call the doctor and luck out. The doctor has an opening today. By the time you arrive, you can barely talk. You feel your neck and think, "Are my glands swollen?" Sure enough, they are. You think of a friend that had swollen glands and remember that he had lupus or was it lymphoma.

Then fear creeps in. "Isn't lymphoma cancer? Oh, if it's cancer then I'm probably going to have to go through chemotherapy . . . my hair's gonna fall out and I'll be sicker than a dog. Man, I hate throwing up! Oh man, I feel like I have to throw up now. It must be that infection." You run to the restroom and throw up.

So, by midafternoon, you went from having a slight headache in the morning to needing chemotherapy for cancer, which, by the way, the doctor confirms you have.

This is how Satan works. He'll put a thought in your head and if you latch onto it, he'll put another thought in your head, and he'll keep doing that until you stop believing his lies or you're dead.

By focusing on each symptom of sickness, you actually manifested them because you spoke Satan's lies instead of the Truth of Jesus already healing you. Peter said in 1 Peter 3:10,

"For whoever desires to love life and see good days, let him keep his tongue from evil and his lips from speaking deceit."

Deceit comes from Satan who is the father of lies, as explained in John 8:44,

"He was a murderer from the beginning, and does not stand in the truth, because there is no truth in him. When he lies, he speaks out of his own character, for he is a liar and the father of lies."

Just as God's character is defined by TRUTH, Satan's character is defined by LIES. He is the opposite of God. Just as God can't be separated from His nature, neither can Satan be separated from his.

If you want bad things in your life, speak Satan's lies. However, if you want good things in your life, magnify God's Truth and manifest it in your life.

Imagine how much pain, fear and stress you could have avoided (not to mention the cost of being sick) if you had just affirmed the Truth; "Jesus healed me and Holy Spirit in me is always taking care of me, so this itty-bitty headache is nothing. I didn't order it, so I'm not going to take it." Then thank Jesus for healing you.

You could be a good disciple of Jesus and help someone else. when you declare you're not going to take Satan's lies, say this, "God, if there is anyone in your kingdom that has this symptom, I release healing to them in the name of Jesus and by the power of His blood. Thank You Jesus for healing us."

Then instead of focusing on symptoms, you look for improvement in your health, because you know that Jesus healed you, and you have called it forth into the earthly realm. (God's will being done on earth as it is in heaven). Sure enough the headache is gone within half an hour.

This does work. I've done it many times.

Here is an interesting thing that happened as I was writing this example. I started feeling what I was writing about and I actually had to take authority over it to keep it from manifesting. That is how powerful our words are.

Our spoken words are even more powerful. These Bible verses affirm that:

From Proverbs 15:4 – "**A gentle tongue is a tree of life, but perverseness in it breaks the spirit.**" What better way is there to suppress your spirit than by speaking Satan's lies?

From Proverbs 18:21 – "**Death and life are in the power of the tongue, and those who love it will eat its fruit.**" Whatever you choose to speak you will reap. If you choose to speak negative things then you will reap negative things. If you speak good things you will get good things. If you speak death you will get death, if you speak life you will get life.

From Matthew 12:36 - "**On the day of judgment, people will give account for every careless word they speak.**" Ouch, there are no other comments needed on this one.

We need to speak words that God would approve of. What would Jesus say? He's supposed to be our example. If He wouldn't say it, then neither should we.

Psalm 19:14 says, "**Let the words of my mouth and the meditation of my heart be acceptable in your sight, O Lord, my rock and my redeemer.**

Maybe it's time to bring back the WWJD bracelets. (**W**hat **W**ould **J**esus **D**o?)

TURN FROM THE WORLDLY WAYS AND REPENT – Sometimes the hardest thing to do is look at ourselves with open minds; see who we really are instead of what we want to see. Before we can turn from our worldly ways, we must first admit we are acting worldly, and thinking with our carnal minds instead of reasoning with our spiritual minds. Proverbs 28:13 states,

"Whoever conceals his transgressions will not prosper, but he who confesses and forsakes them (repents) will obtain mercy."

When we think with our carnal minds, we always look at situations with an egotistical view. Our thinking is self-centered tunnel vision. As a result, we only see what we want to see and not the truth: *how worldly we are.*

We have to be able to reason with our spiritual minds, so that we can look at things with a "big picture" frame of mind. This takes emotion out of decisions we make and will help us to turn away from carnal thinking and hold ourselves accountable to make necessary changes in our lives.

When we are being worldly, we live from our emotions, and often we are fearful. Fear can cause us to make bad decisions, or keep us from acting at all. The next conversation that God and I had is about fear.

I want to talk about the noun form of the definition of fear: a distressing emotion caused by danger, evil, and pain; a condition of being afraid.

When we were having our earlier discussion of fear, you said you weren't afraid of me because you knew me. What is it you know about me that keeps you from fearing me?

Well, I know that You love me, I know You only want what's best for me, just like a good father should. I know it because I can feel it in my spirit, and see it manifested in my life.

I know You will never harm me, You will protect me. I know that your nature is Love, it's who You are. Your love can't be separated from You. I know this because we have a personal relationship.

In other word's you reason this within your spirit. You are not using carnal thinking to be able to know this.

Yes, Father.

The noun form of fear is a condition of being afraid, but what kind of condition is it?

It's a distressing emotion.

That's correct; an emotion. What is the definition of emotion?

1. **A natural instinctive state of mind deriving from one's circumstances, mood, or relationship with others.**

2. **Instinctive or intuitive feelings as distinguished from reasoning or knowledge.**

There are two main points I want to discuss. The first one is "emotion". Emotion is natural and instinctive. It's caused by a feeling. Do you see any problems with this?

Yes, feelings can change based on what's going on around us. Our emotions change as our feelings change, and feelings change as our circumstances change.

So, is emotion based on truth?

No, because emotions can change, and truth is truth, fact, and doesn't change based on feelings.

Look up the definition of "truth."

1. The quality or state of being true

2. That which is true or in accordance with fact or reality.

If truth is fact and doesn't change based on feelings, then that means emotions are not based on the truth, on facts. Emotions are based on what a person perceives to be truth at that time. In addition, as circumstances change, so do the perceptions; hence, the emotions change. Let me give an example:

A man is fearful because he is almost destitute. He doesn't know where his next meal is going to come from, and his truck is going to be impounded for non-remittance of monthly payments. He's scared that he's going to lose everything. He is also very angry. Why? He is angry because of his perceived truth or reality of his circumstances. Here is his perceived reality:

1. *Society hates him because he's not a certain type of person, he's not rich.*

2. *Everyone is out to get him.*

3. *He got fired because his boss didn't like him.*

4. *He doesn't have money to pay for his truck because he doesn't have a job.*

5. The greedy finance company is still going to repo his truck even after he explained why he couldn't make his truck payment.

6. His wife doesn't love him; she took the kids and left.

7. He knows there is no God, because a "loving" God wouldn't let all this happen to him.

His emotions, fear and anger, are based on his circumstances and relationships with others. His emotions are not based on truth. He could know the truth, the real truth, by reasoning.

Let's find out the real truth by reasoning with our spirits:

1. Society doesn't hate him; he's not rich because he never had a financial plan; he never saved any money.

2. Nobody is out to get him; his circumstances are the consequences of the bad decisions he has made.

3. His boss actually likes him; he had to fire him because the man ignored warnings and was late to work more than three times.

4. He doesn't have money because he's not working, but his own actions are what got him fired.

5. The finance company may be greedy, but he missed three payments on his truck, and never contacted the company to work something out.

6. His wife does love him, but she had to leave because he was controlling, angry and overreacted to things, and so self-centered that he spent most of the money on his wants and didn't take care of his family's needs.

If this man would switch from carnal thinking to reasoning with his spirit, he could understand the real truth or reality, which is this:

1. *His perceived truths were based on emotions, not facts.*

2. *His circumstances are what they are because of his own decisions and actions.*

3. *He can change his circumstances by making good choices and taking positive action.*

4. *He can be open to the idea of a loving God, if someone presents that to him, because he knows that his problems are not caused by God, but are the result of his own poor actions.*

I think we all can relate to this story. How many times have our lives gone into a downward spiral because we were thinking with our carnal minds and making choices based on emotions instead of reasoning with our spiritual minds? We need to focus on God's Truth and it will set us free from the constraints of worldly thinking, and from self-induced downward spirals. God continued our discussion,

The second point I want to make is that fearful emotions are caused by danger, evil, or pain. Where does that danger, evil and pain come from?

Well, in this case they come from himself; his bad decisions are what's causing the negative things in his life.

Yes, but why is he making those bad decisions? He's living from his carnal mind and has left himself open to the lies of Satan.

See, that's the problem: when someone doesn't know me, they live their lives from the carnal realm and as a result they live from emotions and not the Truth. I AM Truth. It's my Truth that helps them to reason; to help them see the true reality, not the perceived false reality from Satan.

Now we're back full circle; someone fears me because they don't know me. They project their own self-caused danger, evil and pain onto me, and as a result they think I hate them or, at the least, don't think they are worthy of my love.

That is another problem: they project the world's conditional love onto me, but MY love is unconditional. That's the real truth. That is why someone who fears me has to see my unconditional love before they can trust me, before they can see the truth and reason.

Where are you Church? Why are you not showing these deceived, fearful people my unconditional love? How many of them are you willing to let fall into eternity without me, before you FINALLY stand up and do what you're supposed to do and be who I created you to be: my Ekklesia?

YOU ARE RUNNING OUT OF TIME!!!

(Note: I originally wrote that last line in regular size font and had one exclamation point. God said, "Huh uh. Delete that and make the font size 20 and make it bold and use three exclamation points.")

We are so letting Him down; and the world, too. How many people are lost *forever* because we are not acting like the people we say we are, as it says in 2 Thessalonians 1:9,

"They will suffer the punishment of eternal destruction, away from the presence of the Lord and from the glory of his might."

We must act as God's Ekklesia and address spiritual matters through our physical actions. We must bless the lost, fellowship with them, minister to them by meeting their needs (righting the wrongs) and by proclaiming that the Kingdom of God has come near. This is what Jesus had His disciples do, and it's what He did.

DO ALL YOU CAN TO HAVE A PERSONAL RELATIONSHIP WITH GOD

We cannot be who we were created to be and do what we were created to do until we have that personal relationship with God. We've said that over and over. Our relationship with God is the most important thing in our lives!

Chapter 2 covered the things we need to do to have a personal relationship with God. Here is a list of those things:

- ✓ Spend time with God on a daily basis

- ✓ Let the world go

- ✓ Praise and worship God

- ✓ Ask Holy Spirit for help

- ✓ Keep a journal

- ✓ Use your imagination

- ✓ Pray unceasingly

- ✓ Reread your journals

✓ Do God's will

Reread chapter 2 if you want to review these topics.

Are you walking in the light of God in a strong relationship, or are you walking in the darkness of the world? Remember, as it says in 1 John 1:6,

"God is light, and in Him is no darkness at all. If we say we have fellowship with Him while we walk in darkness, we lie and do not practice the truth."

ASK FOR GOD'S HELP – Never be afraid to ask God for help. He wants you to have a personal relationship with Him, to excel, succeed, and do His will, etc. so ask Him to help you accomplish those things. He is willing to do that. David knew that and said in Psalm 121:2,

"My help comes from the Lord who made heaven and earth."

Ask Him to show you how to do something, to give you the knowledge you need and the wisdom to use that knowledge correctly. Ask questions and then give Him time to answer. Remember, you are working hand-in-hand with Him. He wants you to have an abundant life. He wants to bless you, as it says in Matthew 7:7,

"Ask, and it will be given to you; seek, and you will find; knock, and it will be opened to you."

I was taught that this verse applies to people who don't know the Lord. It doesn't. It's another lie of Satan. Jesus was actually speaking to His followers. Satan doesn't want us to know that there are so many more things available to us to usurp Satan's control over the earthly realm. He knows he has lost, but if he can get us to believe his lies, then he still has some control. The more people believe him, the more control he gets.

STUDY – It's very important to study the Bible, read writings inspired by the Holy Spirit, listen to tapes or videos created by people who do the things you want to accomplish. This is important for five reasons:

1. **You will know the truth**, and be able to discern if what you are reading or listening to is the truth or not.

2. **It will inspire you**.

3. **You will be encouraged.**

4. **You will understand God's will** for your life.

5. **You will recognize just how much God loves you** and cares for you. God said this to me,

It's important to read what my prophets have written; Holy Spirit has inspired them to write what needs said. However, you must also seek me and desire time with me so that I can speak to you on a personal level; for I have specific instruction and guidance just for you; just for each of my people.

Listen to my Holy Spirit. He will guide you in your studies, and will show you scriptures that will either confirm or deny what you are learning. He knows the Truth so trust him.

Put your faith in us. We've put our faith in you!

In chapter 1 – Getting to Know God, under the heading "Truths That Must Be Understood", Faith was the first one listed. That's because nothing of God's will happens in the worldly realm until we call it forth from the spiritual realm. That takes faith, as it says in 2 Corinthians 5:7,

"For we walk by faith, not by sight."

Faith is our belief that what has been accomplished in the spiritual realm can manifest in the worldly realm. That's what gives us the confidence to step out; we're stepping out in faith. God told me,

We are in a huge battle for the souls of humankind. I need your help. Step out in faith. Don't be afraid to ask me for anything.

If you don't have the faith to step out, then you need to reassess your relationship with God. It's your relationship and faith in Him that gives you the confidence you need to be able to step out.

STAND UP TO EVIL – You must remember three important truths to be able to stand up to evil:

1. God has no control over what happens in the worldly realm UNLESS

2. You use your authority given to you when you accepted Jesus as your Lord and savior.

    Never forget that you have authority over Satan's evil plan. Remember, I John 4:4 says,

    "Greater is He that is in you, then he that is in the world."

3. When you don't stand up to evil, you are enabling Satan to carry out his evil plan.

The reason the world is in such terrible shape is that *we*, God's people, are not doing anything to stop Satan. We have enabled him to accomplish much of his plan and control events and people in the world.

BE LITTLE CHRISTS TO THE WORLD – I Peter 2:21 says,

"For to this you have been called, because Christ also suffered for you, leaving you an example, so that you might follow in his steps."

That is our collective purpose; It was through God's love, compassion and grace that we were saved, and it's up to us to follow in Jesus' footsteps, showing God's love, compassion and grace to the world so that others may be saved, as well.

I had a vision of me sitting on Father God's lap. We were looking down at the earth. He spoke these words,

As you sit up here with me, do you see all those lost people down there? I want to wrap them in my Love, as you are now.

I love everyone. I don't want people to die. I want them to come back to me. But the only way for that to happen is if they are righteous, not sinful.

That means we, God's Church must show people His unconditional love so that they can put their trust in Him and accept Jesus as their Lord and Savior. God continued,

I comfort you and give you my Peace so you have the strength and courage to fight the enemy and free the people, so I can rescue them. Be prepared and ready. Remember, with me all things are possible.

Remember: we have the Keys of the Kingdom to open the gates of hell and free people. We are not supposed to be inactive, but active, bringing the light of Jesus into the world. That's God's will.

To learn more about active versus inactive Christians, read Matthew Robert Payne's book *The Parables that May Disqualify You from Heaven.*[12]

It is critical that we are "little Christs" to the world, because we are God's mind, heart, love, arms and legs. He gets things done through us. Actions speak a whole lot more loudly than words.

I had a conversation with Jesus where He explained how all this is possible.

> *My Spirit moves into people when they accept me as Messiah. My aura, my Glory fills them. This is my essence, joined with Father's essence, joining your essence.*

I actually had a vision that God used to show me this:

> I was sitting at the table and I closed my eyes and saw a vision of Father, Son and Holy Spirit sitting around the table with me. The Holy Spirit was sitting in my chair because He lives in me. I was thinking how they were all separate but also together. Then I saw them all rise and fuse together, but right where I was sitting! I actually became a part of . . .a cloud, or essence. I became a part of it; fused with it.

That makes sense, because the Holy Spirit's been teaching me that I am in Jesus, He is in me, and we are both in the Father. And of course, the Holy Spirit lives in me. Jesus continued.

> *We are all one. Our Glory overrides time, because it is eternal, from eternity. Anything in the natural realm is bound by time; however, any circumstance or condition in the natural realm can be changed or eliminated by our Glory.*

> Your eternity dissolves time?

(Chuckling) *My eternity supersedes time. What does supersede mean according to the dictionary?*

To take the place, or move into the position of.

I AM in the first position; top place. My Glory has precedence over time. What does precedence mean?

The fact, state or right of coming before in time, order or position.

I AM first in the order of things because I have the right to be so. I AM before time. I override all.

I looked up the word override. It means:

of a person who has the necessary authority to decide against or refuse to accept a previous decision, an order, a person, etc.

My father has given me authority over the natural realm; actually everything under my feet. I am in the third heaven, so anything below me, including things in the second heaven, where Satan abides, and on or in the earth, is under my authority.

So, if your presence, your Glory is inside us, then why does time still affect us?

Yes, My Glory is from the spiritual realm, but you are human, bound by the constraints of the natural realm; time.

But, You said that Your presence supersedes time . . .

"Yes, but you cannot activate my Glory with your carnal mind. You must fuse your spirit with mine for my Glory to manifest.

Let me ask you a question: How many times in the Bible does it talk about the Glory manifesting in the natural realm without a human being involved?"

Hmm . . . Uh . . . I can only think of one, the actual creation of the natural realm.

That's correct. We created the natural realm through Father's imagination, speaking it into existence. Father can show up in the natural realm, but he can't interact with it because He has no body, no earth suit.

But, if your Glory created the natural realm and supersedes time, then why doesn't your essence, your Glory, automatically manifest into the natural realm?

Because of what happened in the Garden of Eden with Adam and Eve. When Father withdrew Holy Spirit from them, the Glory went, too. They now had to live by the laws of nature for them to be able to function in the natural realm safely. This allowed them to be able to use their carnal minds to cope and find carnal solutions to natural problems and situations.

Their spirits could not affect the natural realm, because they lost the Glory. They were no longer in the first position, no longer had precedence over anything in the natural realm, because the Glory has that position, and they no longer had it. The spirits of people are dormant without the Holy Spirit, so when they don't have Him, they have to rely on their carnal minds.

So, as spiritual beings, we can't operate in the world without our human bodies.

Correct. Humans are of the world, bound by time.

You said that when a person accepts You as Messiah, Your Spirit joins ours.

Yes, they live together, but that doesn't mean they have a relationship. Each person must make an effort to turn his or her switch on and interact with Holy Spirit to have an experiential relationship with Him. Henceforth, to have a relationship with me, my essence interacts with your essence.

I looked up the meaning of the word "henceforth". It means: **from now on; from this point forward.**

Yes. From this point forward, our relationship takes precedence over everything else, as long as you focus on my Spirit, on me. The ideal is to keep developing your spiritual senses to become fully fused with Holy Spirit; like an older couple that reaches the point when they can practically know what the other person is going to do or say before they do it. They know each other that well.

Is that what is meant by going to the secret place?

Yes, it's not a physical place, but a spiritual place where Holy Spirit resides. Look up the meaning of pray.

Prayer is a direct line of a communication process that allows us to talk to God. Praying is like talking to your best friend. It's easy to talk to them because you know they love you unconditionally.[13]

So when your spirit is fused with mine and you are in constant communication with Holy Spirit, my Glory overrides time, and Father's supernatural can intervene in the physical realm. This is available 24/7 to any of our people. That literally means at any time.

Unfortunately, because of Satan's lies, most of our people use their carnal minds most of the time. This is why they "pray" for us to send our Glory and work a miracle. They don't realize they are begging for something they already have. This is why nothing happens. Father can't do anything else, for He's already done everything He can do.

The people must access the Glory inside them by going to the secret place where the Glory is, in the spiritual realm, then grab it and speak it into existence into the natural realm.

Prior to the indwelling of Holy Spirit (after the fall of Adam) humans had to pray to God to send His Glory, then call it forth by reciting God's Word to manifest it. However, now, since we are one with you, the Glory is already available inside of you. You don't ask Father to give it to you, He already did. You still have to call it forth verbally with your carnal voice.

*At the beginning of this conversation, I said that any circumstance or condition can be changed or eliminated by my Glory. In other words, **because we are one with you, you have the necessary authority to decide against or refuse to accept any of the lies from Satan, any circumstance or condition in the natural realm.** You have the Keys to bind and release anything in the natural realm.*

Wow. Imagine how different the world would be if we, your people, could just get a hold of that and run with it.

It would be magnificent!

Jesus just explained how we have the ability to change things in the natural realm. With our spirits connected to Holy Spirit in us, there really isn't anything that we can't do, as long as it's God's will.

If you still need clarity on this subject, I suggest that you read a book written by Kynan Bridges called "School of the Presence."[14] It shows how you can walk in power, intimacy, and authority on earth as it is in heaven.

All this that Jesus told us is the reason we can show God's love to the world. It is also the reason we can show people His miraculous, supernatural power. This is what Jesus and His disciples did. This is important because until people see that God unconditionally loves them, and *has the authority* to override the bad things in their lives, they will never turn their lives over to Jesus.

You may ask, "Well, didn't all that miraculous stuff stop when the last original disciple died?"

I know that is the belief in many churches, but no. It didn't die off when the last disciple died, it nearly died off because of Satan's deceit, his lies that the churches have bought into. Remember, Jesus is our example. We should follow His example.

The Ekklesia accomplishes its mission by doing everything that Jesus did, and more. It's through the supernatural activities that people understand that God is real and can change their lives for the better, just as He has done with the Ekklesia. John 14:12 says,

"Truly, truly, I say to you, he who believes in me will also do the works that I do, and greater then these will he do, because I am going to the Father."

Remember, we are to be little Christs to the world. If Jesus did it so should we.

Father God just told me He wants to say something:

Stop asking me to heal, 'IF IT'S MY WILL.' Of course it's my will! I want every person to have abundant life, not sickness, or poverty or

depression. That comes from Satan. My Son destroyed the works of Satan. And if you don't know what my will is, then you don't know me. If you call yourself a Christian, especially the leaders of my Church, you should already know what my will is. It's written plainly in the Bible and shown to You by the Living Word, Yeshua and explained to you by Holy Spirit. It's ABOUT TIME that my Church wakes up, develops a personal relationship with me and DOES MY WILL! Be my Ekklesia. YOU ARE RUNNING OUT OF TIME.

Remember that Holy Spirit is the one who shows us the Truth and what God's will is, and that can only happen through a spiritual relationship with Him. Again, it is the most important thing in your life!

All through the writing of this book, I could feel the frustration that God has over His Church. We totally must step up to the plate and swing with all we have. People's lives depend on it! Help us Lord!

LET JESUS BE YOUR SHEPHERD - We can't accept Jesus as our Savior without accepting Him as our Lord. Too many people who profess that Jesus saved them, are not willing to make Jesus the Lord of their lives. It is through His Lordship that He becomes our Savior, our Shepherd. Hebrews 13:20-21 speaks of this,

"Now the God of peace, who brought up from the dead the Great Shepherd of the sheep through the blood of the eternal covenant, even Jesus our Lord."

If you don't accept Jesus as your Lord, you will never know God, and you will never do His will. Jesus is the only way to God.

"Jesus said to him, 'I am the way and the truth and the life. No one comes to the Father except through me.'"

Why? Because He's the one that paid the price for your sin. He took *your* punishment upon Himself. He died so you could have life.

126

You can't be half a Christian. It's a commitment, it's a way-of-life thing; you either commit or you don't. Either He's the Lord of your life or He's not. You Choose.

The Bible describes Jesus' lordship as being a good shepherd. Being a good shepherd means watching out for the sheep, protecting them, leading them to green pastures to eat, and knowing each sheep. John 10:14 tells what Jesus says about this,

"I am the good shepherd, and I know my sheep, and they know me." NIV

It means putting himself between the sheep and any danger, as it says in John 10:11.

"I am the good shepherd. The good shepherd lays down his life for the sheep."

Isn't that what Jesus has done for us? He put himself between danger (death) and us, sacrificing himself so we could be saved, as said in Isaiah 53:6,

"All we like sheep have gone astray; we have turned - every one - to his own way; and the Lord has laid on him [Jesus] **the iniquity of us all."**

When God raised Jesus from the dead, He became our shepherd.

To continue to be safe, we must follow Jesus as our shepherd. If we don't, then we are vulnerable. There are many "wolves, lions and hyenas" in the world that would love to grab us and destroy us. We must follow Him to be safe. You can't follow Jesus if you don't know Him; if you don't know His voice. Sheep follow the voice of their shepherd.

At night sheep are kept in a sheepfold. In Jesus' time, it consisted of rock walls and an opening that acted as a doorway. The shepherd would sleep in the doorway. He became the door. If anything tried to get in to the sheep, the shepherd would be awakened and defend his sheep.

If there were more than one flock in the area at night, the shepherds might share the sheepfold. In the morning, each shepherd would call his own sheep and they would follow his voice out of the sheepfold.

I had an interesting conversation with Jesus about this topic. I will type it as it occurred.

> I just need to quiet everything and listen to your voice. You've told us that your sheep hear your voice. Well, that's true if we listen. You are always speaking to us, but we're not always listening. Sometimes we're listening but not hearing your voice. Wait . . . is that even possible, to listen and not hear your voice when you speak? According to what you said, that would be a sheep from another shepherd, right?

> *All sheep listen for their shepherd's voice when they hear someone speak. If it's not their shepherd's voice they hear, they will not follow any other shepherd. My sheep know my voice and follow me . . . but they have to be listening. Some people who claim to be my sheep say they don't hear my voice even when they do listen. That's because they hear a different voice. They are not my sheep.*

> *My sheep hear my voice if they pay attention and listen. If they get distracted and don't pay attention, then they miss my voice and will not be with me when I lead my sheep to green pastures, so to speak. They will miss out on the blessings for*

that day; they're stuck in the sheepfold, because they didn't follow my voice.

Is that a parable about your Church?

Yes. Some of my sheep, my people, miss out on many of my blessings because, they're stuck in the sheepfold, the walls of the building they call 'the church.'

My people are greatly blessed when they follow my voice into the world, for what better blessings could there be than to help make someone else's life better. However, if my people never leave the walls of the 'church' there is no blessing for them or anyone else.

When Jesus said that there could be no better blessing than to make someone's life better, it reminded me of something that occurred in my life years ago.

Every time I see a yard sale sign, it seems as if my car just automatically wants to pull in so I can check things out. One summer, I was at a yard sale and I saw some shelf units that had the hangers on them (The guy had gotten a bunch of stuff from a motel that had been torn down). I bought one for a project I was making.

Months later, about a week before Christmas that year, I decided to take my tithe money and put it into the Salvation Army bucket. As I was driving to the store, another project popped into my mind, and I needed another shelf unit like the one I had purchased earlier in the year.

I didn't know if they would have any more, or even if I could remember which house it was and how to get there. However, I decided to try to find my way back. Surprisingly, I found the place. When I started walking to the door, I noticed that the place looked run down, as if the people there had fallen into some hard times.

I knocked on the door and a woman answered. I explained why I was there and asked her if there were any shelf units left. She said there was and that they were in the back yard. She had thrown everything in a pile and I would have to search through it to find the shelf.

While we were walking to the back yard, she explained to me that one day her husband had taken all their money out of their bank account and disappeared, leaving her and their son with nothing.

When I got to the pile, I found one of the units in good enough shape that I could use it. I also found a couple of other things that I could use. I asked her how much I owed her and she said that I didn't have to pay for the items. I told her that I wouldn't feel right about that, so I handed her a ten dollar bill. You would have thought I handed her the world. She was so appreciative for it. It almost broke my heart.

We said goodbye and I went to the car. As I was getting in, I saw the envelope that had my tithe money in it. There was over a hundred dollars in it. I decided to give it to the woman and her son.

I went back to the house, knocked on the door and she opened it. I explained that I tithed and I wanted to give it to her. I handed her the envelope and she looked inside. She burst into tears and said, "I had nothing to give my son for Christmas, you just made our Christmas!" There are no words to describe how that made me feel, to be able to help her when she needed help the most. That made MY Christmas as well.

Was it a coincident that I thought of the project BEFORE I went to the store and donated my tithe? Was it happenstance that I found the same house? Was it accidental that I showed up, with the needed money, at just the right time? No! What an awesome God we serve!

Tithe money is not your money. It's somebody else's, you just don't know whose it is. However, God knows. He'll get it to the person or organization that needs it. The great thing about tithing is that you have money to help someone when they need help. You don't have to say, "I'd really like to help you but I just can't."

It really is a blessing when you can help someone when they need help the most. But tithing isn't just about money. You can tithe your time, or talents, or even material things.

Jesus continued with our conversation,

> Yes, there are dangers out there, but I will protect my sheep, my people. However, if they never follow my voice they will never learn to trust me. And they will never be able to make a difference in someone else's life; someone who doesn't know me, but longs for the blessings that I can give them through my people.
>
> There are so many people hungering and thirsting for my blessings, for my 'living water.' They don't know where to find what they're so desperately searching for. And since my sheep are stuck back at the sheepfold, those lost souls will look anywhere and try just about anything to fill the void within them. However, that void can only be filled with MY blessings.
>
> Church, pay attention and hear my voice when I speak. Don't get left behind. I need you! The world needs you!

Like Jesus said, hearing His voice is not enough. You also have to follow Him into the world. That is the only way God can get things done on earth. That's the only way you can help others. Praying is important, but doing something is much more important, because you are *living* God's Truth and showing His love to the unsaved. That's how the Ekklesia is so effective.

Remember, God can't do anything in this worldly realm without His people. He literally has to depend on us to get things done here. That's why Jesus had to become human. He needed an earth-suit to interact in this realm. We must open our ears, hear His voice, and follow Him into the world. There should be no ifs, ands or buts about it, no maybes either.

Psalm 23 – **"The Lord is my shepherd, I shall not want. He makes me lie down in green pastures. He leads me beside the still waters. He restores my soul. He leads me in the paths of righteousness for His name's sake. Even though I walk through the valley of the shadow of death, I will fear no evil, for You are with me, your rod and your staff, they comfort me. You prepare a table before me in the presence of my enemies; you anoint my head with oil; my cup overflows. Surely, goodness and mercy shall follow me all the days of my life, and I shall dwell in the house of the Lord forever."**

Dear Lord,

You know me and take care of me. I want to hear your voice and follow you. I want to live your Truth so I can make a difference in people's lives. Please help me. Thank You.

CHAPTER 5

GO INTO ALL THE WORLD

In this book, God has shown His best to show us how to be good disciples of Christ. He's talked to us about how to get to know Him, to understand who He is, truths that must be understood, how to have a personal relationship with Him; our responsibilities, His responsibilities, and how we can connect to Him. He covered important things that we should and should not do; like never abandoning the relationship, doing His will, reaching out to others, as well as why we need to reach out. He's taught us why the Church became so broken and what to do to restore it.

I find it sad and frustrating that He has to step in and teach us what we should have already learned; things that we should have been taught as children. Our parents and teachers could only teach us what they knew. Our pastors taught what they were taught.

BUT NOW IS THE TIME FOR EACH OF US TO SEARCH OUT THE TRUTH AND KNOW GOD'S WILL. NOW IS THE TIME TO STEP OUT IN FAITH AND GO INTO ALL THE WORLD.

In this last chapter, God wants to cover a few important messages for us now today; special messages for a time such as this.

As we get ready to go into the world, we must deal with some issues we and others might have. Until we do, we won't be as effective as we should.

Dealing With Our Hang-ups

God wants to save everyone, because He loves everyone. He wants us to be ambassadors that will reach out to all kinds of people. Unfortunately, there are certain people that we may not want to deal with. There are certain people that we won't approach or even pray for. However, God wants us to understand that we need to see people through His eyes, from His perspective.

THE ENEMY WITHIN – Often times we think that there are people out there that are just too despicable for God to save, that are so evil that we think of them as enemies: Hitler, Stalin, mass murderers, etc. In today's world we might think of leaders that put their own interest above everyone else, even if it means death to thousands.

I was talking about one such person with a friend of mine who asked me, "You don't think God would want to save him, do you?" My answer was, "Yes, He does." It stunned my friend. Here's something that God told me once,

Of all creation, humans are most precious to us, because you were all made in our image. ALL of you are our joy. We desire to have a relationship with every human being and it breaks our heart when people choose to turn away from us, especially those that are lost forever.

Oh, people, please choose life, so that we can bless you beyond measure. We love you!

He will never give up on anyone until the day they leave this world. Even then, He'll love them with all His heart.

In that statement about how precious we are to Him, God didn't say all of you are our joy, **except those that are despicable, or evil**. He said **ALL**. Remember, His love is unconditional and ours should be, too. I know it's hard to remember that God looks at each person and sees who He created them to be. God considers the vilest, most despicable person on earth as beautiful and precious, worthy to be saved.

When Jesus became our Redeemer, He separated us from our deeds. God now bases our value on who we are, not on what we have done. I am so grateful that He did that. We'd be spending eternity in hell if He hadn't. He said,

You cannot separate love from us, because love is who we are; and that is how our Church should be. Love should not be separated from it! If we are in the Church and it is in us, then it should have the same nature, the same character as us.

Come out of Babylon, Church, because, until you do, you are not representing us; our love!

Are we representing God's love? Do we separate a person's deeds from who they are? Or is our value of a person based on what they've done instead of who they are: a precious someone that God created in His image?

The following is a conversation that happened over three different days.

(Part 1)

I was sitting at the table one day and the words "the enemy within" popped into my mind. Then the following words came to mind and I wrote them down, "There is not a single person that ever lived, or will live that is God's enemy. No matter what a person has done, he or she is not an enemy of God."

This surprised me. I told a pastor friend the words that I had written, and I thought it was a message from the Holy Spirit. My friend said that there are verses in the Bible that contradict that, like Romans 5:10. I decided to look up all the verses that mentioned "enemy" and there were a lot. Most were from the Old Testament, but there were some from the New Testament. Moreover, they did indeed appear to contradict what I had written.

I decided to pray and ask Holy Spirit if the words I had written were my words or His. I opened my journal and waited for a response. Again, the phrase "The Enemy Within" came to mind and the words "People are not the enemy of God." So I started writing in my journal. This is what occurred:

> I know the phrase "the enemy within" came from You, but verses appear to contradict that, so which is it: enemy, or not?
>
> *Read Romans 5:10.*
>
> **"For if, while we were enemies, we were reconciled to God by the death of His Son, much more, being reconciled, we shall be saved by His life."** (KJV)
>
> *Look up the meaning of reconciled.*
>
> **To restore friendly relation between.**
>
> *Yes. Notice that in verse 10 the past tense of reconcile is used. That means it's already been done. It happened when Yeshua died and buried the sins of the world with him. Humans have been reconciled to me through the death of my Son. He restored friendly relations between humans and me. Well, if we are friends, then we are NOT enemies. I overcame the enemy, Satan, through Yeshua's actions, and redeemed the lost.*

Remember that God is eternal and lives in eternity. So when Jesus died and our sins were put to death, we were reconciled for eternity, which has no beginning and no end. That means that all of mankind are now friends of God, not enemies, including Adam and Eve.

God continues,

> If people are not my enemies, does that mean they are already saved? No. Look at the second half of Romans 5:10.
>
> **"How much more, being reconciled, shall we be saved by his life."**
>
> The last part of the verse says 'by his life'. You are saved through his resurrection. When Yeshua overcame death, he broke Satan's evil power over the earth; he broke the curse. Yeshua regained my authority by becoming the Redeemer. He redeemed the lost and gave me back to people, through his righteousness.
>
> However, I gave my creation free will. Each person decides if they want to accept that redemption and become my child. If they don't, then they are not mine, not saved. If they physically die before they choose me, they will stay unholy and will spend eternity in the only unholy place there is: hell. Only holy things belong to me.
>
> There are two summations:
>
> 1. Jesus reconciled people when he died on the cross. They can now realize that I'm a friend to them, they do not have to fear me.
>
> 2. Yeshua's resurrected, redeeming life saves people, IF they accept that redemption and I become their Father.

The main point I'm trying to get people to understand is this: humans are not my enemies, so they shouldn't be enemies to my Church. Remember, we are one. Satan is the real enemy that deceives people through their minds. He's the enemy within. He needs to be replaced with me!

Church, it's absolutely critical that you understand this concept. If you think people are my enemies, then you will do anything to destroy them. You will curse them, fight against them and most importantly, will not show them my love. You'll let them fall into eternity without me!

WAKE UP CHURCH, IT'S TIME TO BE MY EKKLESIA!

(Part 2)

That conversation gave me a lot to think about. This was a new concept for me. I don't know if I was told the opposite in church, or if I just assumed it, because nobody ever presented this to me. I was still confused about things, so I asked God to help me understand. This is that conversation.

I now understand what Romans 5:10 means, but other verses seem to contradict your message. Please help me to understand the whole truth about this.

What is the main theme when 'enemy' is mentioned in the Old Testament?

Well, that the enemy will be, or has been destroyed, been cut off, etc.

That's correct. They were enemies to my people, because they wanted to murder my people. Notice that when people called on me, I would step in and help them destroy their enemies, or scatter them.

The point is that they had to call on me because they didn't have any authority over their enemies, because they didn't have my Holy Spirit. Jesus had not yet become the redeemer. I had to come in with my authority to help them. If my people didn't call on me first and tried to fight, they were rousted or defeated by the enemy.

Now let's consider a few things.

1. I AM the same now, before, and forever. If people aren't my enemy now, they weren't then. Notice that on the previous page I said they were enemies of my people. I didn't say they were enemies of mine.

Well, if they weren't Your enemies, why did You destroy them?

They would have destroyed my people. If they had destroyed them, there would be no salvation for the world. My Son would not have been born as prophesied, so there would be no Redeemer. I couldn't let that happen. I love people, ALL people. I don't want them to spend eternity in hell. I want them to spend eternity with me.

I didn't want to destroy anyone. I had to, so hope could flourish. Here is the frustrating thing: If my people would have just put their trust in me and done my will from the beginning, I wouldn't have had to destroy anyone!"

I still don't quite understand how someone can be an enemy of your people without being an enemy of You.

Because of one thing: my people were human, bound by the physical world. If they had a physical death, they would have been separated from me for eternity. They lived by the flesh; they were carnal, relying on their carnal mind, will and emotions, because my Spirit was removed from humans when Adam and Eve sinned.

I am Spirit and eternal. Death has no hold on me; therefore, I have no enemies. What do enemies do? They steal, kill and destroy. I can't be destroyed.

Where do those actions come from? I didn't implant them into humans when I made them. It comes from Satan. He influenced people through their carnal minds and emotions, and then by their own free will, they decided to steal, kill and destroy, becoming enemies of my people, who were under the curse of death.

2. What people fail to realize is that I love every single person that has been or will be born. I even love each person conceived but not born. Each one of you is precious to me! I care for ALL of you as much as I care for Yeshua, my Son. Every single person, born or not, I created in Love. I know everything about every one of you. David knew that and it is mentioned in Psalm 139:14.

"I praise You, for I am fearfully and wonderfully made; Your works are wonderful, I know that full well." NIV

There is nothing anyone can do, or think, that I don't know about. They may try and hide something from people, or even themselves, but they can't hide anything from me. David knew that, too, and in Psalm 139:7-12 says,

"You have searched me, Lord and You know me. You know when I sit and when I rise; You perceive my thoughts from afar. You discern my going out and my lying down; You, Lord know it completely." NIV

David also knew that there was no place he could go that I wasn't already there; even in darkness. (Chuckling) People think they can hide from me in the dark, but there is no dark for me. I AM Light. I can see EVERYTHING.

It was at this point of our conversation that I felt a shift in the atmosphere. I could feel the intensity of God, and when He spoke again, it was with such authoritative sternness that I knew there was no debating or arguing what He said. He was speaking as God Almighty and not as God the Father. It gave me chills when I wrote it in my journal, and it's giving me chills again.

Let me set something straight: every person conceived has a purpose, including you, and I have written a book that contains everything about the lives I have ordained for you all. David wrote of the book in Psalm 139:16,

"Your eyes saw my unformed body; all the days ordained for me were written in Your book before one of them came to be." NIV

So don't believe Satan's lies when he tries to get you, ALL of you, to think that some people don't matter. EVERY PERSON MATTERS – including those in the womb! My babies have a purpose to be born, as said in Jeremiah 1:5,

"Before you were born, I set you apart; I appointed you as a prophet to the nations." NIV

I set each person apart for a sacred purpose before they were born and decreed that they would proclaim my Word and will to the world. If they won't or can't witness to the people they were destined to witness to, those people may not have another chance to hear the good news and choose me; choose LIFE. That is tragic. So, if my babies' lives are cut short and their destinies cut off, I AM NOT PLEASED!!

I think this is one thing that we, God's people, are going to be judged on if we don't stop ignoring the unholy sacrifice of our children. I wish you could feel the fire of His words. It would give you chills, too.

Note: If any of you have ever had an abortion, God still loves you. He has an encouraging message for you about your children, further on in this book.

3. *Since Yeshua's death, the only enemies of my people, those that have chosen me, are Satan and the demons. They should treat NO person as an enemy, because that person is not MY enemy. Why do you think I have told people to love their enemies? And I only use the word 'enemy' because my people think of them as enemies.*

    Again, it's because my people are living from the carnal, not the spiritual. They haven't realized that they are new persons in me; that we are one, and that we are spirit, and live in the spiritual realm.

Remember that the spirit has authority over the natural realm. We as humans would not exist without our spirits. A body needs a spirit to exist, but a spirit doesn't need a body to exist.

I have been trying so long to get my people to realize that they have no human enemies. Why? Because, no person can destroy them. Oh, that person can kill the body, but not the soul, and that is where life is. I have told you not to fear them. (See Matthew 10:28)

THIS IS A SPIRITUAL BATTLE! Ephesians 6:12 explains who our enemies are,

"Your struggle is not against flesh and blood, but against principalities, powers and rulers of the darkness of this age, against spiritual forces of evil in the heavenly places".

*Church, come out of Babylon, come out of the world and live
from my presence as part of my Ekklesia. You have been
ordained to take my good news into the world so that people
can see the Truth and choose me. You can only do that if you
know that each person is loved and valued by me; to know that
they aren't your enemies, because they are not my enemies.*

As I was typing this, it was overwhelming. I feel fortunate that our
original conversations took place over a three-day period. That gave
me time to let things sink in a bit before moving on. Unfortunately,
for you, it's all at once. I would suggest that after you read this book
that you take time to reread these sections, pondering each part
before reading the next.

(Part 3)

I thanked God for revealing these messages to me. However, I still
needed some clarity.

There's still a verse I need clarity on. It's James 4:4.
That's the one that says that whoever is a friend to the
world is an enemy of You.

*You looked up the verse in Strong's Concordance. What is
the word that 'enemy' is translated from?*

**G2190 (ἐχθρός) Transliteration: echthro Orgine:
From a primary echtho (to hate) Definition:**

1. hated, odious, hateful

2. hostile, hating, opposing another

*The original Greek is the true meaning of the message. At
any time, any human (including my people) can be hateful,
hostile or oppose me: It all hinges on their will; the will to*

operate in the spiritual realm, or in the natural realm; reason with their spiritual minds or think with their carnal minds.

Any time a person directs their life through the carnal mind, they have a huge opportunity to oppose me, to NOT do my will, and to NOT live holy. They are very vulnerable to Satan's lies and the snares that he sets.

This happens to my people all the time. Am I going to call them enemies? Of course not, I'll call them deceived; deceived by their real enemy, Satan. And I've already defeated him through my Son. It's a done deal in Heaven. It should be a done deal on earth. And it would be if my people were living from their spirits and calling it forth into the world; my will being done on earth as it is in Heaven.

When will my people wake up and be the light to this world? Yeshua has said that he is done with the aggravating lukewarmness. He's going to concentrate on the remnant and on the new generation that has come. Time is very short, and we simply don't have any more time to sit around and wait for the too-busy-or-too-lazy. . . how did you put it?

(When God asked me that question, He was referring to something I had written in my journal about the Church.)

Hold on; let me look it up . . . Ok. I said, "Why would the world want anything to do with us timid, wimpy, unfaithful, mixed up, distracted, unfruitful fools".

Well, exactly. They DON'T.

Write down what Revelation 3:16 says about this.

"Because you are lukewarm, and neither cold or hot, I will spew you out of my mouth."

What does that verse mean?

When people are born, they do not have the Holy Spirit because they're born in sin. They are NATURAL beings. They are cold, because they don't have the fire of God within them, which comes from the Holy Spirit.

When someone accepts Jesus and believes in Him, they receive righteousness. They receive God as Holy Spirit and they are now SPIRITUAL. Because they have the fire of God working within them, they are hot, and able to do God's will.

When a person has the Holy Spirit of God within them, but has turned off the switch to His power, God's fire, they are neither hot nor cold. They're in the middle, lukewarm. They've become CARNAL, and not able to do His will.

> *Yeshua has reached the point where he's ready to spit out the tepid Christians.*
>
> *Wake up my people! Time is very short. I need you to take your authority back again as my Ekklesia and fulfill your destiny.* **HELP ME SAVE THE WORLD!**

THE FEAR FACTOR – Now that we dealt with our hang-ups about who's worthy to be saved, let's talk about the people of the world and their hang-ups about God.

We won't be very successful going out into the world and ministering to others until we have some insight into why they believe certain things about God.

I. **They think God is wimpy** because His people are. In other words, we have been poor examples of God. We've not been able to do the things that Jesus did and more. He was the best example of God. Jesus was frustrated about this with His own disciples, as mentioned in John 14:9,

Jesus answered: "Don't you know me, Philip, even after I have been among you after such a long time? Anyone who has seen me has seen the Father.

2. **They don't think God has any authority** over worldly things, because we haven't used our authority over anything in the world.

3. **They don't want what we have** because our lives are no different than theirs. We're too worldly. Our lives are as messed up as theirs.

4. **They fear God**. If we don't address people's fear of God, we will not be able to change their minds about God.

The following is a two-day conversation between God and me that deals with the fear that people have of Him

Holy Spirit, you brought up the topic of fearing the Lord. I do not like that term so much, because who wants to have a relationship with someone that instills fear in them? There are verses that say "fear the Lord" and others that say "fear not". Please help me get a better understanding of this.

As soon as I said that, I had a vision of me sitting in heaven with God.

You are here in a vision right now, yes?

Yes, Lord.

Are you afraid?

No.

Why?

Well, because You love me and care for me, even when I do something stupid.

(Chuckling) Do you fear me when you do something stupid?

No . . . I feel guilty, but not afraid.

Why do you suppose that is?

Well, I feel guilty because I know I'm not doing your will at that moment. But, I'm not afraid because I know Your love is unconditional.

Now, imagine if you didn't know me, you only knew my titles: God, Creator of All, The Almighty, The Most High, God That Avenges, etc. Would you come and sit with me?

No . . . I'd probably hide or fall down "as dead" as some people have said.

Why?

Because I'd probably be afraid.

Why? I'm the same then as I am now.

Hmm . . . I guess . . . (chuckling) I'M not the same.

That's correct. So, what has changed with you, in this scenario that causes you to fear me?

Because . . . of who You are?

I AM the same. I AM who I have always been.

Hmm . . . ah, I only know Your titles, which suggest power, might, all knowing, etc. I don't know YOU.

Correct. As a result, you don't understand me. How can a person understand me?

By getting to know You.

How?

By reading the Bible and spending time with You.

But, you said you would hide. How could you spend time with me if you are hiding?

Wow . . . Hmm . . . huh.

(Chuckling) Ok. Let me tell you a story. Once upon a time, the Creator decided to create a beautiful garden, so that he could put humans there to enjoy all the beautiful and wondrous things. The Creator knew that they would love the garden and take care of it.

Humans had everything they needed. They wanted for nothing. The Creator loved them and they loved him. They were spiritual and spent much time together, enjoying each other's company. Everything was perfect. The Creator's heart swelled with joy when they gathered. There was no hunger, no pain, and no fear.

Then one day the Creator went to be with the beloved humans, but they were hiding from him. Of course, they couldn't hide from him, for he could see everything. When he asked them what happened, they told him that they had listened to the serpent. He had deceived them and they had eaten from the tree of knowledge of good and evil. They hid because they were naked and afraid. -- Already, evil had shown its true self. They were already suffering the consequences of sin.

The Creator was so sad. It broke his heart, because He could not be with them anymore. He removed his Spirit from them, because sin couldn't exist with him. The humans were kicked out of the garden, but the Creator still loved them. But now they had to rely on natural laws so that they could operate in the natural realm without his Holy Spirit.

At this point I was crying. Tears were streaming down my face. I couldn't contain myself. It was very odd.

(Crying) I'm so sorry, Father. I feel so . . . sad. My heart aches . . . It feels like it's breaking. What's going on?

We are very close right now. You are feeling what I am feeling.

What . . . How can that be?

Because, we are one; you have my heart.

Oh my . . .

Let's continue the story. The Creator missed having a personal relationship with the humans whom he loved. So he had set a plan in place that would redeem his beloved humans, so that they could have a relationship with him again and not be afraid of him anymore.

The Creator finally found a man after his own heart and told him that down his family line would come the Messiah."

Why did it take so long for that to happen; why not send the Redeemer right away?

Because there had to be prophesies over the ages; enough so that only one man could fulfill all of the prophesies. This was so that people would know that he was the Redeemer, the promised one, when he appeared.

Finally, the day came when all prophesies about him were fulfilled and humans were redeemed by the Creator's Son. The Creator didn't want humans to come back to him out of fear, but out of love. He had given them free will, so he let them decide if they wanted to come back to him. He decreed that all who would accept his Son as Redeemer could have a relationship with Him again. And when they did, the Creator's perfect love cast out their fear.

That's why I have no fear sitting up here with You.

That's right. Now, let's go back to what you said earlier. You said that people would understand me if they got to know me. But if they don't know me, they are afraid of me, so they hide. They know they have sinned just like Adam and Eve knew. I guess they expect me to send an angel with a flaming sword or send a lightning bolt to strike them down.

Here's my question to you: how would you, as a nonbeliever in the scenario, trust me enough to spend time with me to get to know me if you were afraid of me?

Hmmm . . .

Remember, I don't want anyone to spend eternity without me, so this is a very important question.

Well, I suppose someone would have to tell me about You.

Okay, so I'm a person that comes up to you and tells you that God loves you and wants you to spend eternity with him. Would you believe me?

Uh . . . probably not.

What if, as that person, I tell you that it's important to give your life to God because his Son died for you to forgive your sins?

Hmm, I might ask, "What sins?"

Okay, so I then proceed to ask you if you've ever done this or that sin, and you answer yes to any of them. Then I say that if you don't repent and ask Jesus to save you, you will go to hell.

That would strike a note, and I might feel a sense of guilt, but only out of fear, which enforces the image of an angry God. I still won't believe that God loves me, because now I know that I'm not worthy.

So what would it take to get you to give your life to me?

I would have to know that you really did love me and thought I was worth loving. It couldn't just be someone telling me that you loved me. I would have to experience Your love.

Why?

Because then I could trust You and I wouldn't be afraid; well . . . I think.

Yes, because my perfect love casts out fear. Look up the definition of fear.

Noun: a distressing emotion caused by danger, evil, pain; a condition of being afraid.

Verb: I. To regard with fear; be afraid of

2. To have reverential awe of

You are losing your focus. It's late. Go on to bed. We will finish this conversation tomorrow.

(The next day)

Are you ready to continue our conversation?

Yes.

"Okay. When you look at the two definitions of fear in the verb form, you see that the first one describes you in our scenario; regarding me with fear, being afraid of me."

Yes, I see that.

The second definition says to have a reverential awe, in this case, of me. What does that mean?

To have deep respect for.

Would that be possible in our scenario?

No, because I still don't know You enough to respect You.

That's right. Now, not speaking of the scenario, but you right now, do you respect me?

Yes.

Why?

I know You, Your character.

That's correct. For someone to have reverential respect for me, they must know me; my attributes and character. Someone who doesn't know me fears me. Why? Because, deep down, subconsciously, they know they've sinned; just like Adam and Eve. When does the change in a person happen, the change from fearing me to respecting me?"

When they are saved through Jesus?

No, when they see my love applied to them. That happens before they're saved. This is another area my people don't understand. They tell people to repent and to ask Jesus to save them, so that they can see God's love for them. WRONG! They won't give their lives to Jesus until they see my love applied to them! You would know this, Church, if you knew my will. And another thing, they don't have to ask Jesus to save them; HE ALREADY DID!

Here is something for you to ponder: just because someone says they are a Christian, doesn't mean they are. If they still fear me, then they haven't accepted Yeshua as savior and lord. If people have truly given their lives to Yeshua, they won't fear me, they will respect me.

Now, they must have REVERENTIAL respect for me so they can finish the work that I have ordained them to do, the rest of my will. That is a sign of a true Christian. When a person is saved, their life should reflect me, just as Yeshua's life reflected me. That is what sets them apart from the rest of the world. Yeshua made that possible for you.

In the New Testament, when someone says to fear me, they are talking to someone who believes in me. What they are actually saying is to have reverential awe of me. The translators just never made a distinction between the two definitions.

In the Old Testament, when people saw my power or angels, they fell down in fear. The angels had to tell them not to fear. Yeshua even had to tell his own disciples that sometimes.

In the New Testament, after Yeshua died and rose again, people who gave their lives to him weren't afraid of me anymore, because they had my love in them and my perfect love cast out fear – as long as they lived from my Spirit, not with their carnal minds.

Now let's look at my people – my "Church". They aren't seeing any results when they try and minister. Most of them don't know me, because they don't have a personal relationship with me and as a result, they are not doing my will. They think they are, but they are not.

If some do know my will, and try to minister with the wrong approach, they won't see the results that they're hoping for. Instead of showing people my love by blessing them, fellowshipping with them, meeting their physical needs, they throw fire and brimstone at them, "You're going to hell if you don't repent . . . do this, do that, don't do this, don't do that." No wonder people are afraid of me.

Well, I say it's time for my people to humble themselves, pray, seek a personal relationship with me, and turn from their wicked ways. I will hear and heal.

WAKE UP CHURCH! It's time to be my Ekklesia. Seek me first and then all things will be added to you. If you want to be "little Christs" to the world and do my will, then you MUST have a personal relationship with me. That means having reverential respect for me and connecting your spirit with mine, so that we can communicate with each other and you can learn who I really am. Turn your switch ON. Do it now! ***"TIME IS VERY SHORT!"***

Joshua 1:9

"Have I not commanded you? Be strong and courageous. Do not be frightened, and do not be dismayed, for the Lord your God is with you wherever you go."

I thank You, God, for Your love; that perfect love that casts out my fear. Help me to stand firm on Your promises so that I have the courage to do Your will and not my own. Help me, Holy Spirit, to fully awaken my spirit so, together, we can accomplish much. Amen.

Important Messages to Understand and Pass On

There are certain issues that we must understand and then let others know why God considers them important. God has already mentioned one of them.

THE SACRIFICE OF OUR CHILDREN - This on the top of God's list right now. Satan knows that. He knows that young generations are anointed and going to be instrumental in bringing many people to God. They will have an uncanny knowledge and understanding of the things of God. Moreover, Satan will do everything imaginable to wipe out these precious children.

I had a conversation with Jesus. I told Him that I was grateful to Him for loving the children in heaven, and showing them just how important they are to Him; how beautiful and WANTED they are. Most of them probably never felt wanted or valued down here; only abused, kidnapped, raped, torn apart . . . I asked Him to bless each one and thanked Him. Then Father responded,

155

My little ones are filled with joy now. They are so precious to us. My heart swells when I see Yeshua playing with them. He is like a child himself.

I just had a vision of Him falling to the ground and the children piling on top of Him. (Chuckling) . . . sometimes I see them holding hands and circling. One of the children will say something and they all fall to the ground. Perhaps it's a version of "ring-around-the-rosy." However, it wouldn't be the same words. It would be happy words.

God just told me He wants to say something:

For those of you who had an abortion, I want you to know that your children are in heaven waiting for you. They hold no animosity toward you. They are waiting and longing to meet you, and even though we can give them a name, many are waiting for you to give them their names.

Give them their desire. Humble yourselves and repent. I forgive you just as they have forgiven you. NOW FORGIVE YOURSELVES! Choose life and live with me. I want you to spend eternity with me and I can hardly wait for you to meet your children, what a glorious reunion that will be! They are so beautiful and precious.

Wow, that's my hope, too, that you will meet your children. That will be quite a celebration! Those of you that have lost young ones to disease or accidents or murder have the same opportunity to meet your children as well.

Another related topic is the family. God instituted marriage and family. He considers them very important.

THE COLLAPSE OF THE FAMILY – God wants people to value the family. One of the most devastating outcomes of any of Satan's attacks is the disbanding of families. God ordained the family unit, so of course Satan wants to destroy it. I would say that He's done a very good job of it. God wants the honoring of the family restored. We, His Ekklesia, need to promote and uphold the values of family.

This is a dream I had:

> I saw a three-story house and I saw people come out the upper windows and stand on the window ledges; like the family living there had to come out for some unhealthy or dangerous reason. It wasn't like it was an immediate problem, but a growing problem that was getting worse over time.
>
> Then the dream changed to a larger building. More and more people started to come out the windows. The people were having a harder time hanging on, because more and more people were coming out of the windows and space was less and less on the sills.
>
> Someone would fall or get knocked off, then they would try and get back into the building, even though there was something inside that wasn't healthy. But, to be on the ground was even worse. The Holy Spirit interpreted:
>
> *The ground represents the world. The first building represents the family. Conditions in the family are deteriorating and family members are starting to come out to avoid the unhealthy conditions inside. They can't be on the ground because there's worse problems there. Now they are stuck. Their family was protection from the world and the evil things going on there, but now they can't stay in their family because of problems or conditions in it.*
>
> *The big building represents a communal dwelling where people have gone since they don't have a safe home any more. The people in charge of the dwelling has promised to take care of them, so they have some security and some*

protection from the world. However, as more and more people come into the dwelling, there's less provision and protection for those inside. And some of the people causing the problems in the world, start entering the dwelling as well.

It's becoming a hazard to the people inside, so they start to come out of the windows, but there's no place else to go. They're stuck. They want to come out of the unhealthy, dangerous situation, but they don't know what else to do. The situation becomes more and more hopeless.

The people in charge of the dwelling are the agents of the owner of the building. They represent human answers to the world's problems (organizations or governments). However, these systems are controlled by the owner of the dwelling, which in this case represents Satan.

God ordained the family as a way to offer protection and provision, as well as communication to people. A family allows the elders (parents) to provide for the young (children) as well as to teach them, not just about living, but about God and His love for them. The family is representative of God's family and the care He has for His children.

So, a family that stops listening to Father God, or doesn't know Him in the first place, can't operate as a true family should; one that represents His family and His love and care for His children. Ah. They may have some form of love, but not Father's unconditional love.

Exactly. And without His unconditional Love, "love" is controlled by emotions. Ego is now in control. And when that happens, Satan has an open doorway of access to that family.

I see . . . now Satan can harass any member of that family because he now has control.

Yes, but that's not all. Through his "agents", he is also destroying the institution of marriage and family. And as more and more people become less aware of God, there is less and less family structures.

So that means that people have to look for security somewhere else, like government programs and handouts, or worse, criminal activity.

Yes, and that means more "human dwellings", government programs that are becoming more and more inefficient. It also means that the world becomes more violent and dangerous because of criminal activity; people stealing or even killing to get the security they need.

If people would just let God take care of them, life would be less fearful and easier. God wants the people of the world to understand how important families are. They are replicas of His family and how He takes care of us, at least they should be.

This is one of the first things that the Ekklesia addressed when ministering to a person: not just that person's redemption, but the whole family's redemption. That was the point of inception and influence and it grew from there into the workplace.

Security is the main advantage of being a part of a GOOD family:

- You don't have to face things alone.

- Your needs are provided for.

- Your health is better overall.

- You have protection by people who care for you.

- Unconditional love covers you.

Each family member puts the personal needs of the other family members before themselves. No one is excluded.

Unconditional love is what makes that possible: It is God's unconditional love flowing through us. In I Corinthians 13:4-8a is description of the traits of unconditional love.

"Love is patient and kind; love does not envy or boast; it is not arrogant or rude. It does not rejoice at wrongdoing, but rejoices with the truth. Love bears all things, believes all things, hopes all things, endures all things. Love never ends."

We should be showing the world that kind of love. We are supposed to be "little Christs", and that is how He loves. We need to be showing each other that in our families as well.

An earthly family is supposed to be a type and shadow of God's family. Can you imagine how much better the world would be if everyone grew up with the advantages of a good, solid family with a solid foundation in Jesus?

I know some of you are saying, "Yeah, but not all of us were that lucky." Unfortunately, you're right. As the family structures break down, more and more people can say that same thing.

As the amount of single parent families rise, the more poverty there is. Nearly 30% to 50% of children in single parent homes live in poverty.

In 2019, The US Department of Education did a study **of children under age eighteen in families living in poverty, by child's race/ethnicity and family structure; married couple households, father only households and mother only households.**

	Total Averages
Married couple: From 5% to 17% poverty rate.	9%
Father only: From 17% to 41% poverty rate.	24%
Mother only: From 31% to 46% poverty rate.	39%
Source: U.S. Department of Education. Institute of Education Sciences, National Center for Education Statistics	

Most of those children and their families living in poverty are on some form of government assistance

At some point the money will run out as taxes get higher to supply the increasing need. More people will lose their jobs as taxes increase and end up in the system. Taxes will increase again and again to fulfill the need. What happens when more people are dependent on the system than are working to supply the funds needed? The Government will decide who gets and who doesn't.

This is what happens when worldly solutions are used to try and solve worldly problems. Remember in Chapter one, it mentioned that a worldly (carnal) solution was temporary because, even though it might solve an immediate problem, it also creates other problems.

In that chapter it also stated that spiritual solutions were better for worldly problems because it solves the immediate problem, without causing other problems.

It's time to get back to the basics; relying on Holy Spirit's power to guide us and to give us spiritual solutions to worldly problems. We then can develop strong family units, with unselfish desires to help each other and trust in God's ability to take care of us as our loving heavenly Father.

It's time we, His people, start living our lives as children of God and declaring His Truths to the world. It's time we started setting the example! We need to be His Ekklesia.

These are verses for the family:

Couples: **"For we are members of [Christ's] body, of His flesh and of His bones. For this cause shall a man leave his father and mother and shall be joined unto his wife, and they two shall become one flesh."** (Ephesians 5:30-31) KJV

Fathers: **"But if anyone does not provide for his relatives, and especially for members of his household, he has denied the faith and is worse than an unbeliever."** (1 Timothy 5:8)

Mothers: **"She watches over the affairs of her household and does not eat the bread of idleness."** (Proverbs 31:27) NIV

Children: **"Honor your father and mother, then you will live a long, full life."** (Exodus 20:12)

(Note: I'm not saying that women can't work outside the home, but they still must watch over the affairs of the household. They must be aware of what is going on.)

I had a vision in which I was in heaven sitting with Father again. Jesus was sitting beside us. This is a short conversation I had with Him.

Hi, Yeshua. I love You.

I love you, too. I adore you!

Thank you for accepting me and for choosing Father. It's a pleasure to have you as part of our family. There was a great celebration when that happened.

For ME?

Yes. We all love you up here. We, the saints, the angels, and the heavenly beings had a marvelous celebration.

(Sighing) Why is it so hard for us to see ourselves as You see us?

Father spoke next.

It's because of conditioning by the world. Just know that we love you with all of our being. Oh, how precious you all are to us! We miss our people when they are away from us. There is an empty spot, a void, when one of my children has turned off their access to me. I miss them so much . . .

Do not forget that we are all connected through my Holy Spirit, and when one of my children is far from me, I feel it. The connection is still there because of what Yeshua accomplished. However, my child's spirit is dormant; the essence is in limbo. I miss interacting with my child.

I don't think that most of us really understand that we are literally a part of God's family. He has adopted us and we have all the rights as a child of His, as 2 Corinthians 6:18 says,

"And I will be a father to you, and you shall be sons and daughters to me, says the Lord almighty."

WHY THE CHURCH NEEDS TO WAKE UP – I was reading about some of the evil things going on in the world. God initiated this conversation.

Are you starting to realize why I need my Church to wake up and be my voice to the world?

Yes, Father I do. I've known for a long time that there were people who are opposed to You and Your plan for this country and the world. I've known for decades. I read an underground newspaper, forty years ago, that gave warnings about these people. It talked of what they are up to; their real agenda for the world. I just never realized how deep and far-reaching their tentacles have grown . . . I guess a lot can happen in forty years.

Yes, that's my point: Forty more years for Satan's agenda to be played out, and forty more years of corruption and deviation from the Truth. My Church has been silent too long.

Multiply your forty years by millions; millions of my people not doing anything; not even praying. I realize that you and others never knew the whole truth and had no idea what to do about what you might have been told or had read, but I knew. I know exactly what to do, when to do it, and how to do it. I know everything.

Unfortunately, because of corruption in religious churches, my people are blind and dumb, deceived and/or shell-shocked if they heard of the truly evil and deviant things going on. But, praying is so simple, so easy . . .

But, we haven't even done that. We've become the flavorless salt, the tepid water, lukewarm as You talked about in Revelation; worthy to be spit out.

But, I'm not ready to spit out my Church, not quite yet. I need my Church. There is a very long and hard road to travel, a huge battle to win. Yes, there are people to pray for, situations to deal with and specific skirmishes for each of my people to fight.

This is why I have ordained this book; to teach you, my people, who you are and what you need to do.

Yes, there are specific deviant people in a worldwide cabal that must be stopped, but you must never forget the root of it all — Evil, which comes from the spiritual realm. You must fight with your spirit, not your soul. Remember, people aren't the enemy, Satan inside their minds is.

Equip yourselves with my armor and my Word, and always be listening for Yeshua's commands. He is my general.

In Ephesians 6:14-17, it explains what God's armor is:

"Stand firm then, with the belt of truth buckled around your waist, with the breastplate of righteousness in place, and with your feet fitted with the readiness that comes from the gospel of peace. In addition to all this, take up the shield of faith, with which you can extinguish all the flaming arrows of the evil one. Take the helmet of salvation and the sword of the Spirit, which is the Word of God."

Don't get discouraged about what's going on in the world politically. That's not your battle, other than to pray and support my people that I have put in government positions around the world. I AM already taking care of that with the help of certain Ekklesia members; 'draining the swamp' as people like to say. However, this is a worldwide swamp!

Don't question the time factor. This is a worldwide battle and it's going to take many strategic skirmishes to overcome the enemy. It's going to take stealth and cunning like never before in the history of humankind.

Just trust us, and all of you do your part. Fight your skirmishes, which deal with the people, not their evil doings. I AM taking care of that. Remember, I love all of them. You show them my love. Let them know there is a better way; a way of peace and joy and rest for their weary souls. Matthew 11:28 says that,

"Come to Me, all you who are weary and burdened, and I will give you rest." NIV

This is not an easy battle, because the enemy is fighting back. He's bombarded my people with his lies and soulish attacks. You are not strong enough to fight him in the soulish realm. Remember we fight a spiritual battle.

Unfortunately, most of my people are trying to fight from the soulish or worldly realm, because they have no personal relationship with me. They are carnal; their switches are turned off.

You must activate your spirits, turn on your switch so that your spirit, fused with my Spirit, can access the power that he offers. You, then, will be strong enough to overcome anything.

Don't get sidetracked. Don't join someone else's battle, we're handling those. You stay focused on your battle. And if you get weary, call for reinforcements. I have plenty of angels to help; twice as many as Satan had, by the way.

Keep the faith, my Ekklesia. Let your righteous anger flow. Treat every problem, every roadblock as a life or death situation, because it is. It's a huge battle over the souls of humankind; of light over darkness, good over evil; the ultimate life or death situation.

Stand up my Church. Join my Ekklesia, and fill the gaps between what is and what should be. And pray until 'what is' becomes 'what should be.' Be quiet no longer. You are my people, my family, ACT LIKE IT. TIME IS VERY SHORT!!

Matthew 28:18-20

"Go therefore, and make disciples of all nations, baptizing them in the name of the Father and of the Son and of the Holy Spirit, teaching them to observe all that I have commanded you. And behold, I am with you always, to the end of the age."

Dear Jesus,

Thank You for making it possible to become a part of Your family. Help me to never forget who I am, in You. I will do my best to make disciples of others and to bring them to You so that they can be a part of the family, too. I love You.

The Ekklesia - Special Forces

THE EKKLESIA'S BATTLE PLAN - As part of God's Ekklesia, it's important to understand the battle plan; after all, it is a battle we're fighting. It's a spiritual battle which requires spiritual wisdom and weapons to fight.

Again, this book isn't an in depth study about the Ekklesia. You do need to study more so that you know and understand its role as 'the body of Christ', so that you, as a member have the knowledge and *wisdom* to be an effective soldier for God.

This is an overview of the plan.

The main mission of the Ekklesia is to heal unreconciled human realities in the earthly realm. These realities are found in Ephesians:

Chapter 2 – Ethnic divisions

Chapter 3 – Religious disunity

Chapter 4 – Ministerial competition

Chapter 5 – Discord between genders

Chapter 6 – Family strife and Marketplace injustice

These are the battlegrounds. God is our Supreme Commander. Jesus is our Commander in Chief, and He assigns us our missions through the Holy Spirit. That is why our switches must be turned on. They are our walkie-talkies.

Our missions are to be followed in a strategic order to make sure that nothing is missed: one thing leads to another.

1. Bless the lost

2. Fellowship with them

3. Minister to them by meeting their needs (righting the wrongs) which require miracles oftentimes.

4. Proclaim that the Kingdom of God has come near.

Remember that this is what Jesus told His disciples to do AND SHOWED THEM how to do it. He's not back at Command Central, He fights alongside us!

Notice that the "preaching" part is last on the list. We do the first three to gain peoples' trust and to show them how much God loves them. Then they are ready to hear the Good News and give themselves to the Lord.

THE EKKLESIA'S PURPOSE – As the Ekklesia Special Forces, our purpose is to go behind enemy lines and seize his territory and clear it out.

We first have to know where that territory is and then understand the layout: what and who is there.

The enemy territory is wherever unholiness is. It's made up of the unredeemed, unrestored lives and actions of people who are living from their worldly senses and not with their spiritual senses, as well as unredeemed authority, families, governments, schools, cities, states and nations.

Because it doesn't have God's Living Water flowing through it, it is a swamp. Here is part of a conversation I had with God.

> *Satan's territory is a stagnant swamp because there is no movement of fresh water to stir things up. The mire just keeps getting deeper and deeper. You, as my Ekklesia, must get things flowing by building channels that bring my fresh Living Water into the swamp, and to flush out the stagnant water.*

> *A channel must have walls or banks for the water to flow, and those banks cannot be too far apart. You can't make the channel too broad.*

> I read in Ed Silvoso's book EKKLESIA,[15] that the banks are built with principles that lay down strong foundations. They are not projects or programs, but a trans-culture, trans-generational and trans-denominational lifestyle.

> *Yes. Since my Kingdom is a spiritual kingdom, everything is based on spiritual principles and not on physical projects, programs, or anything in the natural realm.*

> *In the physical realm, there are boundaries, restrictions, scientific laws, human opinions, ethnic groupings, hierarchy positions, religious snobbery and of course satanical influences.*

169

Yeshua understood that the Ekklesia's mission must be based on holy principles instead of worldly things that have restrictions, because someone somewhere would be left out. It is my will that ALL people be a part of my Kingdom.

This is why Yeshua chose the ekklesia model over the religious church model. Everyone is welcome no matter their heritage, what culture they come from, what age they are, whether they are male or female, their ethnic background, race or nationality.

But in Matthew 15:24 Jesus said he came to speak to the Jewish nation, that You chose them to be Your people.

"He answered, 'I was sent only to the lost sheep of the house of Israel.'"

Yes, my nation. However, He also blessed some who weren't Jewish, because of their faith in Him. It is faith that brings people into my Kingdom.

You have to understand, and most of my people don't, that when someone accepts Yeshua as their Redeemer and Lord, they are adopted into my family; into my nation. It is one nation, under God; Mine.

It is okay for the Ekklesia to have programs or projects to meet the needs of people, but my principles are the foundation of the banks that bring my Living Water into each person's swamp, as well as each city's swamp, each nation's swamp, and to the world's swamp. My Special Forces build those banks, those walls.

THE EKKLESIA'S METHOD – Since our purpose is to build banks to create a channel, we have to have a method that is reliable and doable. Since there are two walls, we have to have a two-fold method.

In Ed Silvoso's book, he explains what the Ekklesia needs to do to accomplish its purpose: To bring God's Living Water into the spiritual swamps of the world. The following summation comes from that book.

The first bank is made up with five pivotal paradigms. A paradigm is a model of something or a pattern. They are:

1. The WHAT – Disciple nations as well as individuals.

"Go ye therefore, and teach all nations, baptizing them in the name of the Father, and of the Son, and of the Holy Ghost." (Matthew 28:19)

2. The WHY – For atonement secured redemption for the marketplace, which is the heart of the nation.

3. The HOW – Labor is treated as worship.

"Whatever you do, work heartily, as for the Lord and not for men, knowing that from the Lord you will receive the inheritance as your reward. You are serving the Lord." (Colossians 3:23-24)

Since we are to be full time ministers, we turn our jobs into places of worship.

4. The WHERE – We use the Keys of the Kingdom to lock and unlock the gates of Hades, binding and releasing in order for Jesus to build His Church where those gates stand, using the unsaved people we've set free.

5. The WHAT FOR – We eliminate systematic poverty, in all four of its dimensions: motivational, relational,

material and spiritual. Poverty is the consequence of sin and is empowered by the Gates of Hades.

In Luke 4:18 Jesus said the following,

"The Spirit of the Lord is upon me, because he has anointed me to proclaim good news to the poor."

What would represent good news? Well, It would be compassion for the hopeless, friendship for the friendless, food for the hungry, clothes to the naked, and wealth to the poor. Poverty was the first tangible social manifestation of the Gates of Hades on earth after the Fall of man.

This paradigm opens doors with government officials because we have something valuable to offer: solutions to help eradicate systematic poverty. Jesus' promise to the poor is an integral part of the Ekklesia's agenda. There was no poverty in the Ekklesia.

The second bank is made with Prayer Evangelism. The definition of evangelism is this: **The spreading of the Christian gospel by public preaching or personal witness.** (It is the personal witness that God needs His people to do. We are to take Him into the world.) In prayer evangelism, we take God into the spiritual atmosphere surrounding a person, or city, or government through prayer.

Discipling a city or nation begins with changing the spiritual climate at point of inception, and then progressively continuing to change it. For godliness to increase, ungodliness must decrease and this requires a change in the nation's spiritual climate. This is why we need a personal *spiritual* relationship with God.

We've left control of the spiritual climate in cities and nations in the hands of the devil. This is evident when we look around at the mire of sin, criminal activity and the crushing weight of hopelessness.

We must take control by prayer evangelism and living out the five pivotal paradigms for transformation, which is taking God's Kingdom to the people. It must be a lifestyle!

Deuteronomy 31:8

"It is the Lord who goes before you. He will be with you; He will not leave you or forsake you. Do not fear or be dismayed."

Dear Lord,

I'm so grateful that you are leading from the front lines instead of the rear. You are a true leader, one we can put our confidence in and trust. Thank You for giving me the chance to fight alongside of you. Help me Holy Spirit, to become an effective member of the Ekklesia. I want to take God's Kingdom into the world.

I pray this under Christ's authority, amen.

Encouraging Words

As God's children, we have to stand up against evil. However, Satan is not going to give up easily. That can overwhelm us sometimes, because we are human after all. We are Satan's enemies. However, If we stay connected to Holy Spirit and keep our eyes focused on Jesus, we will stand firm, because God has promised to take care of us and to protect us. We do not have to fearful as it says in Isaiah 41:10, and in Psalm 46:1,

"Fear not, for I am with you; do not be dismayed, for I am your God. I will strengthen you and I will help you, I will uphold you with My righteous hand."

"God is our refuge and strength, a very present help in trouble."

God is ever-present, *always* here. Though we may abandon Him sometimes, He will NEVER abandon us!

David understood that. He knew that God was always with him, even when he messed up. He wrote a song about this. It is written in 2 Samuel 22. If we have made Jesus our Lord then this should be our song too.

DAVID'S SONG IS OUR SONG – 2 Samuel 22. David fought many battles in his life, and God delivered him from them all. He sings of this in verses 2-3,.

"The Lord is my rock and my fortress and my deliverer; the God of my rock; in Him will I trust; my shield and the horn of my salvation, my high tower and my refuge, my Savior; Thou savest me from violence." (KJV

These verses tell us that the Lord is our rock, unmoving and stable. He is our strength and we should trust Him. He is our Savior; when we call upon Him He rescues us.

Before we were saved, death surrounded us. But Jesus heard our cries for help, and He has rewarded us according to our righteousness. Verse 25,

"Therefore, the Lord has recompensed me according to my righteousness, according to my cleanness in His eyesight." KJV

Remember that when we gave ourselves to Jesus, we became righteous, because He traded his righteousness for our sin. We are now clean in God's sight. It's a little different for us than David.

David's righteousness was based on what he did because he was under the law of Moses. God told me this,

My Son fulfilled the Old Covenant – the Law – It was based on doing or not doing something. You live under the New Covenant of Grace – undeserved favor.

Our righteousness isn't based on what we do, but on what Jesus did for us.

David sings of what he did in 2 Samuel 22:22-24. He tells us about what God is to us and what He does for us, and how we are able to get things done. In verses 29-32 he sings about how Jesus is our light.

"For You are my lamp, O Lord, and my God lightens my darkness. For by You I can run against a troop, and by my God I can leap over a wall. This God, His way is perfect; the word of the Lord proves true; He is a shield for all those who take refuge in Him. For who is God, but the Lord? And who is a rock except our God?"

In verses 33-37 David sings about how God is a refuge and shield.

"This God is my strong refuge and has made my way blameless. He made my feet like the feet of a deer and sets me secure on the heights. He trains my hands for war, so that my arms can bend a bow of bronze. You have given me the shield of Your salvation, and Your gentleness has made me great. You gave me a wide place for my steps under me and my feet did not slip."

The Lord is a light that illuminates our way through the darkness of this world. We can run across and leap over obstacles. His way is perfect and His Word proves it. We can take refuge in Him because He is our shield. He is our Lord, our solid foundation and our protection. He equips us to climb over the rocky areas of our lives, and sets us on high. (We sit at the right hand of God with Jesus.)

He trains us for the spiritual battles which we must fight and gives us the strength we need. He shields us with His salvation, and HIS humility on the cross, and what He did for us, has made US great! This gives us confidence to keep fighting and not stagger or give up. Father God appreciates what Jesus did for us. He told me the following,

Anyone who comes and resides in my presence, I can fill up with my Glory because they are willing to be an open vessel that I can use for my purposes. I give them to my Son as a reward for all his suffering and his willingness to do MY will and not his own.

I made him King over my Kingdom and his concern isn't about power, but a desire for all people to be a part of my Kingdom. And when someone makes the decision to enter my Kingdom, and I can present them to Yeshua, his heart swells with gratefulness and joy. Oh, how glorious it is to feel his joy!

LIKE-MINDEDNESS WITH JESUS – Because of what Jesus did for us, and because we have given our lives to Him, we have His mind. We *should* have His mind, according to Philippians 2:5,

"Let this mind be in you, which was also in Christ Jesus:"

We have to be like-minded when it comes to Jesus. If we've made Him Lord of our lives, then we must think like Him and do what He did. Remember, He is our example as mentioned in Philippians 2:1-2,

"If there is any encouragement in Christ, any comfort from love, any participation in the Spirit, any affection and sympathy, then complete my joy by being of the same mind, having the same love, being in full accord and of one mind."

We are united with Him through the Holy Spirit, and think like Him. So what did Jesus think about and do when He walked the earth? He encouraged, comforted in love, had fellowship with Holy Spirit, had compassion and mercy. He did nothing out of strife and conceit. He was humble; putting other's needs above His own. He didn't just look to His own interests, but also to the interests of others. This is what we need to do as it mentions in Philippians 2:3-4,

"Do nothing from selfish ambition or conceit, but in humility count others more significant than yourselves. Let each of you look not only to his own interests, but also to the interests of others."

Reread that paragraph above the scripture. Now, let me ask you a question. What was said about Jesus in the above paragraph that makes people Hate Him? Nothing. He treated people like we all want to be treated. But yet many hate Him. . .Talk about being deceived.

Philippians 2:7 says that He became a servant,

". . . but emptied Himself, by taking the form of a servant . . ." He served others.

"He humbled Himself . . ." as said in (Philippians 2:8.

These are the things we should be thinking of and focusing on, because we became one with Him and the Father.

I am so grateful that we don't have to rely on our own carnal minds to do these things. I believe it would be impossible. Because we now have the mind of Jesus, we can go out into the world with confidence, knowing that we are representatives of Him and are equipped to do the things we need to do.

PSALM 91: A TWO-PART PROTECTION PLAN – God and His people have a partnership. We work together to carry out His divine plan. He has promised to take care of us, but we also have our own responsibilities as part of that promise.

Psalm 91 is known as the protection Psalm. In fact, people have been using this Psalm for hundreds of years to activate supernatural protection. When you recite this Psalm, treat it like a prayer. Make it personal as well, by inserting your name or the name of someone for whom you are praying.

I'm going to insert us or we instead of a name. As you read, please take note of several things: This protection plan covers every possible danger. Notice that it says that it's His faithfulness to us that is or shield, not our faithfulness to Him. He will always be faithful to us, but we can't say that we have always faithful to Him. Notice that this is a 24-hour protection plan and lastly, pay attention to what God says He will do if we love Him.

This is Psalm 91:

"We who dwell in the shelter of the most High shall rest under the shadow of the Almighty. We will say of the Lord, "He is our refuge and our fortress, our God in whom we trust." Surely, He will deliver us from the snare of the trapper and from the deadly pestilence. He shall cover us with His feathers, and under His wings, we shall find protection; His faithfulness is our shield and wall.

We shall not be afraid of the terror by night, nor of the arrow that flies by day; nor of the pestilence that stalks in darkness, nor of the disaster that strikes at noonday.

A thousand may fall at our sides and ten thousand at our right hands, but it shall not come near us. We will only look on with our eyes and see the reward of the unholy.

Because we have made the Lord, who is our refuge, even the Most High, our dwelling, no evil shall befall us, no disaster will come near our dwelling; for He shall give His angels charge over us to guard us in all our ways. They shall bear us up in their hands, least we strike our feet against a stone. We shall tread upon the lion and the cobra; the young lion and the serpent we shall trample underfoot.,

Because they love Me I will deliver them; I will set them on high, because they have known My name. They shall call upon Me, and I will answer them; I will be with them in trouble, and I will deliver them and honor them. With long lives, I will satisfy them and show them my salvation."

The first part of this Psalm is our responsibilities in this promise. What are they?

OUR PART:

1. Live in the shelter of the Most High, which puts us in the Almighty's shadow. That means we're very close to Him.

2. We declare that the Lord is our refuge (a place of safety) and a fortress (no one gets in to harm us) and that He is our God in whom we trust.

   A. We declare it to God as a pact.

   B. We declare it to ourselves as a reminder of His protection, and as a personal code.

   C. We declare it to others as a witness to God's love and protection.

3. We trust Him to continue to take care of us, just as He did for forty years for His people in the desert.

GOD'S PART:

1. To deliver us from:

   A. Satan's traps

   B. Deadly diseases

2. To protect us

   A. Like a mother hen that calls her chicks and they run to her and hide under her wings. (For anything to get to us, they would have to go through God first.)

   B. By His faithfulness to be our shield and wall

BENEIFITS OF THIS PROTECTION - Because He delivers us and protects us, we need not be afraid. Remember, His perfect Love casts out fear. This gives us boldness because we have confidence in Him to take care of us.

Things we won't be afraid of:

1. Anything that people can throw at us; attacks that are physical or verbal

2. Any spiritual attacks from Satan

3. Any sickness or disease

4. Any natural disasters

This also means 24 hour protection: night, morning, evening, day. We never have to worry if He's going to show up no matter what time of day or night it is.

Even if thousands are falling all around us, we are protected. We will only look at the destruction, not experience the consequences of people who won't put their trust in the Lord and live under His protection.

When we put our trust in God:

1. No evil will befall us

2. No plague will come near our homes

3. His angels will guard us in all our ways. They will lift us out of the way of trouble.

Because of this 24/7 protection that we have, we can now fight the enemy with confidence and trample down his attacks:

1. The bold in-your-face lion type attacks

2. The sneaky, surprise attacks that we don't see coming (like a cobra attacking from the bushes)

3. The quick, jabbing type of assaults (like a young lion that's still learning how to fully take down her prey)

4. The deceiving attacks in our minds (lies and half-truths from the serpent - Satan) that keep creeping up on us.

We will stomp down all these types of attacks because we have God's authority over these things as long as we live under His divine protection, by staying very close to Him in a personal relationship.

Because we love Him, He declares His promises to us:

1. He will deliver us.

2. He sits us on high with Him and Jesus – we are a part of His family because we know Him. (We have a personal relationship with Him.)

3. He will answer us when we call out to Him.

4. When we're in trouble, He will be with us.

5. He will deliver us from that trouble.

6. He will honor us.

7. He will give us long life.

8. He will show us His salvation.

WHAT AN AWESOME GOD WE SERVE! He says,

Don't give up! Don't lose heart! Don't be afraid! We are one with you. We appreciate you. We bless you.

Peggy Joyce Ruth has one of the best studies on Psalm 91[16]. It is a very down-to-earth and simple study. I highly recommend it. She has many testimonies from people who've been supernaturally protected. It is very fascinating and inspiring.

Isaiah 54:17

"No weapon forged against you will prevail, and you will refute every tongue that accuses you. This is the heritage of the servants of the Lord, and this is their vindication from me," declares the Lord."

Dear Lord,

Thank You for protecting me, and neutralizing the weapons used against me. Together we can stop Satan's evil agenda. Thank You for Your strength and courage. I am grateful for them. Amen.

A Message to Non-Believers

Primarily, this book is for people who have already believed in and accepted the sacrifice that Jesus made on their behalf, and has become part of God's family.

However, for those of you who may be reading this book but still don't know the Lord, or haven't given your life to Him, you need to know that God loves you and has a special message for you.

This is His message:

You may not know me, but I know you. I created you out of my Love, and you are precious to me. You will always be precious to me, whether you spend eternity with me, or not. I do hope that you will join my family as my adopted child, and spend eternity with me. I have so many wonderful things to show you, so many blessings that I want to give to you.

I just want you to know that my Kingdom is a spiritual kingdom not bound by the constraints of the world. You do not have to live under the oppression and deception of worldly boundaries. Nothing is impossible for me. There is no earthly problem, or person, that has authority over me. I AM the Creator.

If you are tired and weary, hurting and lonely, sick and depressed, come to me and let my Son carry your burden. Give your heart to Him and My Spirit will give you faith to trust me. He will show you the Truth and it will set you free, free to soar! Oh, how I long for that. I want to see you soar. I LOVE YOU!

IT ONLY TAKES THAT VERY FIRST STEP

It only takes that very first step
To change your life forever.
And, it will absolutely be
Your most important endeavor.

In this world that makes no sense,
Things are so confusing and blurry.
You tell yourself, "Don't think! Don't think!"
Because it causes such strife and worry.

But deep inside you know what's true.
You just finally have to admit it.
And when you do your life is changed
And you're saved, right where you sit.

Your life is redeemed and whole again
Because of the price that Jesus paid.
Now *He* will be watching over you
And no longer will you be afraid.

So live your life under His control
And you'll avoid an eternity of sorrow.
You'll rise and meet Him in your new home
And have a lasting, joyous tomorrow.

— Patricia Welsh
© November 2016

God's Final Message in this Book

I want to take care of people. There are terrible things coming to the earth because of Satan's hold on the earthly realm. There are certain people that have given their lives over to Satan and want to control everything in this world, and they are willing to do anything to get control. They are willing to sacrifice anyone to make that happen.

As a result, they are willing to hold back necessities such as money, water, food, electric, gas, etc. They want to create chaos and many people could suffer and die. Are you prepared? Your spirit lives on, but where will it spend eternity?

I have promised to take care of people, however, they must accept redemption from Yeshua, and be willing to do my will and let me direct their lives. I took care of my people in the desert for forty years. I fed them, kept their shoes and clothing from wearing out, and I protected them.

I want to do the same today. If my people want to survive the after-effects of the chaos and unholiness in the world today, they must humble themselves, pray, seek my face and turn from their wicked ways. I will heal their lands.

Having a personal relationship with me is the only way you can know my will and trust me to take care of you. You must have me in your hearts so that you can be 'little Christ's to the world and help them survive as well. It's my presence, my Glory inside of you that makes it possible for my people to be who you were created to be and do what you were created to do — everything that Yeshua did and more.

You must be able to do miracles, like multiplying food or water, healing the sick, (because there are going to be more diseases to contend with), and raising the dead. You must be willing to go where I need you to go, to whom I need you to show my love. It could be the last chance for that person to be saved from death, which is separation from me for eternity.

There is going to be violence and chaos. It's imperative that My people listen to what I'm saying. DO NOT focus on what the world is saying! You'll get discouraged and give up. That's exactly what Satan is trying to get you to do; AND IT IS WORKING! Don't listen to the news! Read the headlines to know what's going on so you know what to pray for, but DON'T read the story. Listen to me to know what I am going to do about it, or what you need to do. Remember, I AM the Truth.

Listen to My prophets because I have given them the Truth. They may not know all the details, but I will not do anything until I tell my prophets first so they can tell my people. Remember, I can't do anything on earth until a human speaks it first. Thereby, my people can prepare, pray and be ready to stand. I am working with certain people right now and we will accomplish what needs to be done! So focus on ME, not the world!

For the Lord God does nothing without revealing His secret to His servants the prophets. (Amos 3:7)

If my people do what they were ordained to do, and pray with AUTHORITY, then this time of turmoil and judgment can be drastically reduced.

Are you, my people, willing to take a stand and cut evil off at the root? Are you willing to stand up to Satan's lies and tell him, "You have no authority here, I do. You are not going to do your evil here, not on my watch! "

Are you going to stop living from the worldly realm and start living in the spirit so that my will is done, so that my love is passed on? The future of the world is at stake.

Are you willing to be a part of my Ekklesia? Are you willing to take the Keys of the Kingdom and bind evil and loose people. This is your last, greatest chance to make a difference in people's lives, including your own.

I want to save a billion people in the coming worldwide revival. I can't do it without you.

Don't let us down!

"TIME IS VERY, VERY SHORT!!!

I Timothy 6:11-16

"Pursue righteousness, godliness, faith, love, steadfastness, gentleness. Fight the good fight of the faith. Take hold of the eternal life to which you were called . . . "

Dear Lord,

I am so grateful that You have not given up on me, that You consider me worthy to carry out Your will. Thank You for teaching me Your Truth, so that I can be free. I am willing to be a part of Your Ekklesia and stand with You and fight the good fight, until Jesus comes back again. I love You, honor You and praise You, in Jesus' precious name. Amen.

I STAND WITH YOU

Lord, I stand with You in these trying days.
I know You are still King.
You show us love in all Your ways.
I let my praises ring!

Now's the time for us to declare,
In voices loud and strong,
"Our light will shine, so darkness beware,
We're here to right the wrong!

We won't give up, no matter the cost,
Our strength comes from above.
We will prevail for the sake of the lost
Through God's redeeming Love."

- Patricia S. Welsh
© January 2021

CONCLUSION

Well, this has been a fascinating and wondrous adventure for me. I'm still amazed how Holy Spirit has inspired me to write God's messages, to me first, then to you. He told me a few times that I should just keep learning and doing until it was time to release me. I never really understood what that meant, and He wouldn't tell me. He just wanted me to step out in faith and trust Him.

Now, over a year later, I finally understand. Mostly, I understand that He had to teach me the things that He needed to convey to you. I had to know about and understand the meanings of His messages before I was able to have confidence that what I was typing in this book was the truth. I believe that I would have given up if He hadn't spent the last year teaching me these things; it would have been too overwhelming.

I asked Him this morning what He wanted me to include in this "Conclusion". He told me to include the things that touched my heart the most, so I am:

- I am amazed at how much He yearns for a personal relationship with all of us. He doesn't say, "Well, ok, let me know when you're ready, I'll be around." No, He's constantly fighting for that, always finding ways of letting us know how much He loves and cares for us. He's always pursuing us, not just waiting around for us to make that commitment.

I never understood that a personal relationship with Him is most important to Him. Now, I realize that it has to be the number one thing. That relationship is what makes everything else possible; everything from salvation to trusting Him, to loving and helping others, to taking authority over Satan and his demons and to accomplishing God's miraculous works. That's the meaning of Matthew 6:33,

"Seek Ye first the kingdom of God, and His righteousness; and all things will be added unto you . . ."

- Another thing that touched me deeply was the fact that when we give our lives to God, we become adopted children of His. We are royalty. This almighty and powerful God becomes our loving, compassionate, doting Father, who would do anything for us, if we would just let Him.

  God has bestowed on us all the inherited benefits that are, by right, ours as His children, including His authority to represent Him in this world. When we go out into the world knowing we are royal children of His, representing Him, Satan and his demons take notice. Humans may snub or ridicule us, but Satan knows that when we show up as heirs of God, He has no power over us. Humans may not understand that, but our enemy does.

- I never quite understood what the righteousness that Jesus exchanged for our sin really was. Now I know that it is the actual presence of God, through Holy Spirit. Jesus traded Father God's presence for our sins. Do you realize how big of a sacrifice that was? Jesus was willing to give up His relationship with Father God, so that we could have a relationship with Him.

  That must have been so devastating to Him. To lose that connection meant that when He died in our place, He took upon Himself our hopelessness, our anguish. For the first time in His existence, He felt forsaken.

The amazing thing is that He could have stopped the whole thing at any time, but He didn't. That is the absolute greatest example of unconditional love ever!

- One of the biggest misunderstandings I had was the correlation between the spiritual realm and the worldly or natural realm. I didn't realize that our spirits are who we really are and that they are eternal. I didn't realize that we are actually living in both realms at the same time, through our spirits in the spiritual realm and through our souls in the natural realm.

Our souls contain our physical senses, our emotions and our wills. Our wills are what we use to switch from one realm to another. It is our switch to turn on the power of Holy Spirit, and to turn off that power as well.

- I finally understand why the "church" is so ineffective in ministering to the unsaved; why the outcome is so different than in Jesus' day and why certain scriptures never made sense to me. We have not been operating as an ekklesia, which is the only way to minister to the secular world. That is the answer to my question "Is there something more?"

- However, the most astonishing thing I learned, is the fact that God is NOT in control of this world. I think that is Satan's most effective lie ever. That has allowed God's Church to become lazy. "We don't have to worry. We don't have to do anything because God is in control." If God was in control, this world would look a whole lot different than it does now!

The most amazing thing of all is the reason God doesn't have control of this world. He can't interact in the physical world because He has no physical body, no earth-suit. He can only have His will done on earth, as it is in heaven, through His people, who have the means to interact with the world, who have the earth-suits.

He is spirit, and that is why he needs us to have a personal, *spiritual* relationship with Him. We must commune with Him through our spirits because a spirit can only commune with another spirit. We are the mediators between humankind and God.

If we don't like what's going on in this world, then we need to take the authority we received, and change the circumstances. We cannot pray to God to do something, because He can't. He's done all that He can: given us everything of His that we need to do His will on earth. It won't get done otherwise.

• I now understand why He had me write this book: to teach us His Truth so that we can be free to be true disciples of God, as His Ekklesia, the Church as it was meant to be. There is a lot God must accomplish, but only if His Ekklesia does it.

Will you join with me and become a part of God's royal army, His Ekklesia. We can't be passive any longer. We must stand together, united and committed to God's cause. We must fill the gaps in the line, and then advance together as an unbreakable force, pushing the enemy back until he can't go back anymore!

Thank you for reading this book. My hope is that it was as much an inspiration to you as it was for me; however, not just inspiration, but revelation as well. Now, let's take this message, and His Love, out into the world; start rattling those keys! Let 'em know were coming! Shalom!

Numbers 6:24-26

"The Lord bless you and keep you; The Lord make His face to shine upon you, and be gracious unto you; the Lord lift His countenance upon you, and give you peace."

Dear God,

Thank You for never giving up on us, and for the messages in this book.

I declare, that Your will be done on earth as it is in heaven!

I declare that no weapon of the enemy will prevail against me.

I declare, that as Your child, I will stand with You and use the authority and the Keys of the Kingdom that You have given me to cut evil off at the root and change the spiritual atmosphere in peoples' lives.

I WILL SHOW THEM YOUR LOVE!

GOD'S HEART IS BROKEN AGAIN

When Jesus bore the sins of the world,
As he hung upon that tree,
He cried to his father in distress,
"Why have you forsaken me!"

God and sin cannot co-exist,
So He had to turn away.
For the very first time their connection was lost
And both hearts were broken that day.

The torn flesh, the punctures and the pain
Were nothing compared to what He lost.
Fear, despair and utter hopelessness
Overcame Jesus as he paid OUR cost.

When we don't have a connection with God
We suffer a major loss.
We live our lives in fear and despair,
Just like Jesus as he hung on that cross.

And if we die and leave this world
Without answering God's call,
His heart is broken all over again,
Because He loves us best of all.

- Patricia S. Welsh
© November 2016

ACKNOWLEDGEMENTS

The first acknowledgement must be for God. This is His book after all. I just wrote the words that He gave me. His love and care for the Church, His Ekklesia, as well as the people in the world, is the reason this book exists. I thank Him for letting me be a part of it and give Him honor, praise and glory for all He has done on our behalf, and for never giving up on us.

I thank all of the people that had a hand in making this book a reality. I greatly appreciate your input and help. I deeply appreciate those of you who have prayed for the successful completion of this project.

A special thanks goes out to Rosann Pavlov who has been, not only a staunch supporter, but also my proof reader and confidant. I say to you, "The spiritual journey I've been on for the last year has only been possible because of your friendship. I don't think I could have completed this book without your support. You have lifted my spirits many times. Thank you very much."

Last, but not least, I thank all the disciples, the Ekklesia, now and in the past that have spread God's message across the world, especially our Lord and Savior, Jesus Christ. "You are my Rock!"

ENDNOTES

1. *How to Commune with God* [Christianity], Wikihow, last modified: April 22, 2020, https://www.wikihow.com/ Commune-with-God-(Christianity)

2. Philip Wijaya, *What is Righteousness*, last modified December 16, 2019, https://Christianity.com/wiki/christian-terms/what-is-righteousness.html

3. Tony Meyer *Pushing the Boundaries in Christ: Living Supernaturally* (2020)

4. Troy A. Brewer, *Redeeming Your Timeline* (Shippensburg, Pa.: Destiny Image Publishers, 2021).

5. Editorial Staff, *What is Holiness?* Last modified: May3, 2019, https://www.christianity.com/wiki/christian-terms/what-is-holiness-what-can-be-holy.html

6. The Collingsworth Family, Southern Gospel Singing Group, www.thecollingsworthfamily.com

7. *Oxford Languages Dictionary*, s.v. "power", 2020

8. Matthew Robert Payne, Conversations with God: Book I (Litchfield, IL.:Revival Waves of Glory Books & Publishing, 2016

9. https://EzineArticles.com/expert/ Matthew_Robert_Payne/43219 Submitted On February 26, 2007

10. J. Warner Wallace, *The Difference Between Killing and Murdering*, last modified: July 18, 2013, https://coldcasechristianity.com/writings/the-difference-between-killing-and-murdering

11. Come and See Foundation (2023) *The Chosen* (1.5.0) [Google Playstore]

12. Matthew Robert Payne, *The Parables that May Disqualify You from Heaven* (Litchfield, Ill.: RWG Publishing, 2021

13. *What is Prayer?* All About Prayer, 2021, https://www.allaboutprayer.org/what-is-prayer.htm

14. Kynan Bridges, *School of the Presence: Walking in Power, Intimacy, and Authority on Earth as It Is in Heaven*(Shippensburg, Pa.: Destiny Image Publishers, 2017)

15. Ed Silvoso, *Ekklesia: Rediscovering God's Instrument for Global Transformation* (Bloomington, Minn.: Chosen Books, 2017

16. Peggy Joyce Ruth, *Psalm 91: Real Life Stories of God's Shield of Protection And What This Poem Means for You & Those You Love (Lake Mary, Fla.: Charisma House, 2007)*

STUDY MATERIALS

Ekklesia

Tim Kurtz. *Leaving Church Becoming Ekklesia.*

Other Works by Ed Silvoso: 2017 *Ekklesia-Group Guide. Minnesota:* Chosen Books; 2002 *ANOINTED FOR BUSINESS.* 2002 Study Guide, California Regal Books; 2007. *TRANSFORMATION.* Minnesota: Chosen Books.

Prayer and Evangelism

Andrew Womack, 2007 *A BETTER WAY TO PRAY,* New Hampshire: Harrison House Publishers.

Ed Silvoso, 2000, 2018. *Prayer Evangelism,* Minnesota: Chosen Books

Charles Bello & Brian Blount, 2011. *From the SANCTUARY to the STREETS.* Coaching Saints Publishing

Family

Ed Tandy McGlasson. 2013. *THE FATHER YOU'VE ALWAYS WANTED.* Michigan: Baker Books.

Ed Silvoso. 2001. WOMEN: God's Secret Weapon. California: Regal Books

Karen Jenson Salisbury. 2015. *Helping Your Children Make Right Decisions (CD)*.

Supernatural

Kynan Bridges. 2021. *Unlocking the Code of the Supernatural: The Secret of God's Power in You*. Pennsylvania: Whitaker House.

Sid Roth. *It's Supernatural*. TV Show. North Carolina: Messianic Vision.

SCRIPTURES USED

Church/Ekklesia
Matthew 28:18-19
Revelation 21:23-24
Ephesians 1:22
Acts 19:10
Matthew 16:18-20
John 14:12
Colossians 3:9-11, 23-24

Commandments of God
Ephesians 5:18
Exodus 20:3-17
Matthew 5:28
John 14:23
John 15:10

Creation
Genesis 1:26

Discipline/Judgment
Hebrews 12:11
2 Thessalonians 1:9

Evangelizing
Revelation 1:19
Habakkuk 2:2

I Peter 4:10
Exodus 9:16
Philippians 2:4
Mark 6:4
Jeremiah 1:5
Matthew 5:16
Mark 16:15

Faith/Trust
Hebrews 11:1
Hebrews 11:6
Psalm 86:15
James 2:14, 17
James 4:17
Proverbs 3:5-6
2 Corinthians 5:7
Philippians 4:13
Psalm 139:14
Psalm 139:7-12

Family
Colossians 3:9-11
I John 3:1
Ephesians 5:30-31
I Timothy 5:8
Proverbs 31:27

Exodus 20:12

Gifts/Talents
1 Corinthians 12:7-10
Romans 12:5-7
Ephesians 4:11
1 Peter 4:11

God's Character
Psalm 25:8
1 John 4:8
Psalm 11:7
Psalm 89:14-15
Proverbs 2:8
Isaiah 55:8-9
Exodus 9:13

God's Will
John 6:40
1 Peter 2:15
Luke 11:2
Amos 3:7
Matthew 15:24
Ecclesiastes 3:1
John 6:38
Matthew 7:21

Goodness/Greatness
Philippians 4:19
Isaiah 41:13
Jeremiah 10:6
Nahum 1:7
Jeremiah 29:11
Philippians 4:19
Psalm 121:2

Psalm 8:3-4
Luke 6:9
Isaiah 54:17
John 14:12
Philippians 4:19

Health /Healing
Matthew 12:13
Isaiah 53:5

Holy Spirit
Acts 1:8
Ephesians 3:16
1 Corinthians 7:10
Romans 12:5-7
Ephesians 4:11
1 Corinthians 12:11
1 John 4:4
John 14:26

Humbleness/Repentance
1 Corinthians 11:31-32
James 4:10
2 Chronicles 7:14
Psalm 25:9
Revelation 3:19
Proverbs 1:23
1 John 1:9
Proverbs 28:13
Acts 3:19

Jesus/Messiah
Matthew 12:10-13.
John 8:36
1 Peter 2:21, 24

Isaiah 53:5
John 10:14
John 10:11
Isaiah 53:6
Ephesians 1:22
Philippians 2:7-8
Hebrews 13:20-21
Acts 14:12
Psalm 23

Joy/Rest/Peace/
Psalm 126:5
Philippians 4:7-9
Matthew 11:28-29

Judgment
Matthew 12:36
Proverbs 28:13
2 Thessalonians 1:9
Matthew 7:17
Revelation 3:16

Love
1 John 4:8
Philippians 2:1-2
Philippians 2:7
1 John 3:1
1 Corinthians 13:4-8

Prayer/Praying
Matthew 6:7
1 Thessalonians 5:16-18
Isaiah 28:23
John 1:13

Prophecy
Philippians 2:7
Revelation 5:1-3, 6-7, 13
Revelation 8:2

Protection
Exodus 14:14
Psalm 91
Joshua 1:9
2 Samuel 22:2-3, 25, 29-37
Ephesians 6:14-17
Deuteronomy 31:8
Matthew 6:33
Psalm 50:15

Righteousness.
Psalm 11:7
Psalm 34:15, 17
Psalm 18:20
Romans 5:10

Satan/Enemy
1 John5:19
1 Peter 5:8
John 8:44
Matthew 10:28

Seeking the Lord
Isaiah 28:23
Luke 11:28
1 Chronicles 16:11
Psalm 37:4
Matthew 7:7

Sin

James 4:17

Romans 1:32

Spiritual Living
Mark 6:4
Mark 16:15
Isaiah 55:8-9
Philippians 2:2-5
Luke 16:10
Jude 1:1
1 Peter 3:10
Colossians 3:2

Words
Proverbs 15:4
Proverbs 18:21
Psalm 19:14

Worldliness
1 John 5:19
1 John 2:15-17

Strength/Energy/Power
Philippians 4:13
Isaiah 41:10
Isaiah 40:31
Isaiah 41:10
Psalm 46:1
Psalm 18:2-3
Psalm 18:28

Teaching/Training
Psalm 32:8
2 Timothy 3:16
Luke 6:40
Luke 16:10

Truth
John 8:32
John 16:13
1 John 1:6

Ungodliness/False Prophets
Jude 1:4, 12
Matthew 7:15

INDEX

U

W

Y

ABOUT THE AUTHOR

Patricia Welsh was born in Dover, Ohio during a time when most people in the USA went to church, most people professed to be Christians and Social Security had barely gotten started. Prices were low and taxes were low because people depended on each other and God to take care them instead of a run-away social service system. If there was a need, you filled it, or found someone who could. She states,

"Over the decades, less and less people have attended church, many people who profess to be Christian, don't live like it, and Social Security and social services have become unsustainable juggernauts and way too many people look to the government to take care of them instead of God. Many people have no idea who their neighbors are, let alone help them."

Patricia grew up in Amish country in a small rural town called Winfield, Ohio where the Grange and church were the social center points of the neighborhood. She gave her life to Jesus as a teenager and attended church most of her life, and even though Patricia has the deepest respect for the ministers who were sincere and loving, deeply caring about their "flock", the messages were incomplete, modern day, watered down versions of God's Truth. The ministers taught what they were taught.

Patricia knew there had to be more, and in 2009 started on a quest to find what the "more" was. Gratefully she has found it in a personal relationship with God as part of His Ekklesia. Now her goal, with Holy Spirit's help and inspiration, is to help others find that "more" as well, especially God's people, who have the same doubts, confusion and questions that she once had.

www.ingramcontent.com/pod-product-compliance
Lightning Source LLC
Chambersburg PA
CBHW021622120626
46545CB00001B/354